LIVING WITH
WEALTH

WITHOUT

LOSING YOUR
SOUL

A Pastor's Journey from Guilt to Grace

STEVE PERRY

WITH STEVE HALLIDAY

RosettaBooks®

NEW YORK 2016

Lyrics from Scott Wesley Brown's song
"Blessed to Be a Blessing" are used by permission.
All Scripture quotations are from the *Holy Bible,
New International Version*, unless otherwise noted.

RosettaBooks editions are available to the trade through Ingram
distribution services, ipage.ingramcontent.com or (844) 749-4857.
For special orders, catalogues, events, or other information, please
write to production@rosettabooks.com.

∞ This paper meets the requirements of
ANSI/NISO Z39.48-1992 (Permanence of Paper).

First edition published 2016 by RosettaBooks
Cover and interior design by Corina Lupp

Library of Congress Control Number: 2016933747
ISBN-13: 978-0-7953-4855-6

www.RosettaBooks.com
Printed in the United States of America

To my beloved wife of forty years, Susie, who willingly and faithfully journeyed and struggled with me to discover how God wanted us to live with the wealth He entrusted to her.

And also to her parents, Hal and Jeanette Segerstrom, who modeled for Susie and her family a life of selfless generosity.

CONTENTS

FOREWORD

The important subject of wealth touches everyone, and at many levels. Consider a few examples:

A spiritual issue. Wealth brings up questions about the blessings of God, our stewardship, and our responsibility. We all want to appreciate what He has provided and to enjoy the good life He has designed for us: "This is to My Father's glory, that you bear much fruit" (John 15:8). At the same time, financial resources can often add angst to our spiritual lives as we ask, *Am I living in the right way with this wealth?*

A career issue. A person's financial status will deeply affect what job, career, and work sectors he or she will choose. Money provides great job opportunities and career paths unavailable to the financially strapped. And in the wrong settings, it can also hinder one's work ethic and ambition.

A relational issue. Wealth touches all of our important relationships: our marriages, children, dating life, parents, friends, and colleagues. It can enhance love and intimacy, but at the same time it can also contribute to painful relational conflicts and even alienation. When I coach members of families of means, my primary task is often to help guide them to choices that enhance good communication and health while at the same time preserving the strategic and legacy value of the family's money. They often have to engage in difficult but important conversations so that everyone gets on the same page.

An emotional issue. As a psychologist, I have always felt struck by the reality that no one ever experiences the topic of wealth in a neutral or nonemotional fashion. It is evocative. It brings up all sorts of feelings, including guilt, ambivalence, happiness, embarrassment, and confusion. While it can create a sense of profound joy, it can also contribute to sleepless nights of anxiety.

Wealth is important to us all—but it is also important to God. The Bible has a great deal to say on the subject, as you will discover in this book. So we *must* understand it. That is why Steve Perry's book is such a winner.

Steve not only knows the topic objectively, he has lived the topic for decades. Steve has navigated a solid and loving marriage with his wife, Susie. They have raised great kids and grandchildren. He has had a successful career. He has established a worldwide philanthropic foundation. And he has forged many deep and long-lasting friendships, including the one he and I share.

But the true uniqueness of this book is that Steve has experienced both sides of the wealth equation, since he was not born with it. He grew up in a middle-class American family and knew nothing of great capacity until he married Susie, who comes from a family of great means. This single reality, combined with his own perceptiveness, together have provided Steve with a potent viewpoint that you won't find anywhere else and which adds greatly to the value of his book.

I can remember many conversations with Steve when he first starting working on the ideas in his book. He felt a call to help those with wealth move beyond the guilt of thinking of it as a burden and instead to normalize the reality, enjoy the blessing, and strategically utilize it to make the world a better place for God's kingdom. To accomplish this, Steve delivers his message in several effective ways:

It is thoroughly biblical. Steve is a formally degreed theologian and was a full-time pastor for many years. The depth and precision of his biblical insights are illuminative and spot-on. As I read the material, I saw many passages in a different light than I had before.

It is vulnerable. As a writer and a reader myself, I am constantly into books. One of the things I enjoy about a great book is that the writer brings me into his own vulnerability and authenticity. I am drawn to that book because it identifies with my own weaknesses. I don't have a lot of time to read books that come from a position of invincibility and "I've got it all together." Steve takes some significant risks of self-disclosure in these pages that will engage you. As you read about his feelings and thoughts about becoming instantly wealthy the day he married Susie, you won't be able to put the book down. I know I couldn't.

It is challenging. Steve's book has a purpose: he wants to encourage and help people of wealth to establish a balanced viewpoint so that they can be healthy themselves and serve God in more optimized ways. Any good book must stretch us to think and behave in new ways that develop and mature us. This one delivers.

It is practical. The most helpful books have clear constructs as well as useful action steps. You will find here many nuggets of practical wisdom along with realistic suggestions of how you can make life work better with wealth.

It is funny. You will find no attitude of rigidity or extreme seriousness here. Steve is a funny guy and deals with a serious topic in a way that makes you enjoy entering his world. It's as if you're sitting on the back porch of his home with a cup of coffee, randomly talking about life and laughing with him about its peculiarities.

I can say without reservation that this is the best book I have ever read on living with wealth in a healthy, biblical, and God-honoring manner. You are in for a treat!

Blessings,
Dr. John Townsend
New York Times best-selling author of *Boundaries*
Leadership expert and psychologist
2015

INTRODUCTION

O nce upon a time, a faithful, God-fearing Jewish boy fell in love with the girl of his dreams. They talked about getting married and anxiously waited until after college graduation to be joined together in wedded bliss. He knew nothing about the girl's family except that she called them farmers.

They got engaged on graduation day, when he finally met her family. He felt very happy to know that her lovely parents would become his in-laws. He loved them and he felt warmly welcomed into their family.

Then one day, his future father-in-law decided to show him the farm—and to his great surprise, he discovered that his fiancée's family raised pigs.

Can you imagine his cognitive dissonance?

I don't have to imagine it, because I lived it.

To be sure, the details of my story differ from those of the parable. I'm not Jewish, for one thing, and my wife's family raised lima beans, not pigs. But I felt every bit of the cognitive dissonance that overwhelmed the young man in the parable.

I'll offer more details later, but for now, you should know

that I grew up in a middle-class home and always assumed I'd marry a girl from similar socioeconomic circumstances. It never occurred to me that I'd fall in love with someone from a very different background. I never envisioned any kind of money in my future. Furthermore, I had no desire for it—quite the opposite, really. I felt the same kind of revulsion toward having a lot of money that a devout Jewish boy would feel about owning a pig farm.

So when Susie and I got engaged and her dad revealed to me that their lima bean farm—twenty-two hundred acres in the middle of Orange County, California—would soon start generating great wealth, I felt an indescribable flood of cognitive dissonance.

I had always expected to be poor. Now it seemed I would be wealthy.

I had always looked down on the rich, seeing their money as spiritual poison. Now I would be drinking from that cup.

I had always felt spiritually superior because of my poverty. Now I feared the unknown of what my new reality would bring.

In this book, I want to chronicle a part of my journey, not because I imagine my story to be so important, but because I hope it may help other Christians of capacity—believers in Christ who, by virtue of God's grace and diligent effort, have the financial means to creatively further God's kingdom—to come to grips with their own situations. It took me about two decades to fully see that God had led me on this journey and that he had a purpose in sending me down this path. I hope that by reading my story, you might make the trip in far less time and better enjoy the journey.

A Journey Toward Understanding

I confess that the title of this book might seem misleading. You may have assumed this book is about the journey of a Solomon-like character who had an aha moment when he recognized the meaninglessness of wealth. Or maybe you thought it was about a man who pursued the lusty promises of wealth, only to lose it and then disown the folly of it all.

That is not my story.

On the contrary, *Living With Wealth* is about a man in passionate nonpursuit of wealth who suddenly found himself immersed in great wealth. It's about a bewildering journey to discover God-honoring contentment while living in a state of plenty. I have realized over the years that most people believe that having plenty is the path to contentment in life. Wealth, they believe, means: No worries! No cares! No sorrows!

That is not my story, either.

> *Wealth brings many more temptations, responsibilities, and concerns than most could ever realize.*

Solomon realized that the more he had, the more he had to be responsible for and the more he had to worry about how those who followed him would use his wealth. Just read the book of Ecclesiastes.

Wealth brings many more temptations, responsibilities, and concerns than most could ever realize. But ultimately, the biggest burden (at least, for me) was finding out how to become a faithful steward of all that God had entrusted to me. I knew all too well that "To whom much is given, much is required" (see Luke 12:48). This burden became a constant barrier to contentment for me. I could not come to peace about my wealth, and so I constantly badgered myself with hard questions:

"Am I spending too much on myself?"

"How much does God expect me to give?"

"Is it wrong to enjoy one's wealth?"

"What, exactly, is enough?"

While many theories attempt to describe how someone should live with wealth, I have come to realize that most theories about Christians and wealth champion a one-size-fits-all approach. And that fact caused me to ask two of the most important questions to fall within these pages:

- Does God really want us all to walk the same path and carry the same exact cross?
- Is it really possible for the wealthy to live in righteousness and humility before God and others?

After years of wrestling, I finally came to the bedrock question underneath all the others: Is it really possible for the wealthy to live righteously before God? Those on the religious left often demonize wealth as the corrupter of society, while those on the religious right often view wealth as the corrupter of one's soul. But if Scripture describes the wealth of Abraham and other godly men as a blessing from God, then can it also become a blessing for us, whether that wealth came to us through hard work, luck, or family fortune?

That is the question that has driven me for many years. Perhaps it has crossed your own mind, too. In the following pages, we'll set out to find some satisfying answers.

1

A DIVINE COMEDY

M y father always told me that it's easier to marry a rich girl than a poor one. While I'm sure many fathers have given their sons similar advice, I had no idea that marrying a rich girl in real life would pose as many challenges for me as it actually did.

As I've said, I never intended or even desired to marry a rich girl. After a profound encounter with Jesus in 1971, it was the furthest thing from my mind. I had somehow developed a piety that believed poverty is next to godliness (see the next chapter), and as the son of parents with modest means, I grew up in a twelve-hundred-square-foot tract home, built in the '50s. I had no connection to people of wealth. Zero.

After I graduated from high school, I took some classes at a junior college and a state school, and then got a clerking job at the FBI. When I left that job after a year (to the dismay of my father) in order to attend Bible school, I sold my new car to pay for my education—a major sacrifice for a car guy. But I didn't fear the sacrifice. I feared only that God would call me to do one of two things: (1) Be a pastor or (2) be a missionary. The thought of marrying a rich woman hadn't even occurred to me, but if it had, it would have been number three.

> *I had somehow developed a piety that believed*
> *poverty is next to godliness.*

With visions of sacrificially serving God filling my head, I packed my few belongings and headed off to California Lutheran Bible School, a tiny institution in the heart of Los Angeles with a student enrollment of 120. The experience transformed my life. Not only did it help to strengthen my spiritual legs, but the closer I drew to God, the less resistant I became to the two vocations I feared most. By my final year at CLBS, I felt ready to become a missionary. I led the missionary prayer group at school (all three of us) and went on a six-week mission trip to Nicaragua in the summer of '73. I was ready to *go!* But as much as my heart wanted to be a missionary, I knew I lacked the most important element: the call of God.

Not knowing what to do next, I decided to return to college to finish my degree, in part to honor my father. I already had so many college credits that it would take me only a year to earn my degree at Azusa Pacific College (now university). I enrolled in the fall of 1974.

Back then, the school held tri-weekly chapels, where I often found a seat for myself at the back of the auditorium. But this day was destined to be different. With homecoming approaching, the college decided to parade the female candidates for homecoming queen before the student body. Of the ten finalists, one in particular stood out. She had long brown hair, a big, bright smile, and wore a '70s-style granny dress. During my two months at the school, I had never seen her lovely face. I leaned over to the guy sitting next to me and said these exact words: "Now, *there* is a girl you can take home to Mother."

About a month later, for a Christian Education class, I had to attend the Greater Los Angeles Sunday School Convention at the Anaheim Convention Center. While breaking for lunch, I decided to view the displays of several Christian organizations. My friends wanted to go off-site for lunch, but I jokingly replied, "I think I'll hang around here and see if I can find some girls." Knowing me as they did, they just laughed, because they knew that when it came to girls, I was more talk than action.

During my meanderings, I came across the Azusa Pacific booth—and suddenly froze in my tracks. There *she* was, working the booth. I wanted to introduce myself, but at that moment she was speaking to a prospective student. I loitered, pretending to look interested as I leafed through random brochures, just waiting for an opening. In a few minutes, she turned her attention my way. With the same bright and cheery countenance I had seen before, she greeted me. She had no idea who I was, since I lived off campus with four other guys who, like me, had graduated from CLBS.

"Are you interested in going to Azusa?" she asked. Her voice sounded as sweet and cheery as her face (and hasn't changed one bit, years later).

"Um, no," I replied, "I already go there." We made the normal introductions and conversed about the school and our majors. We discovered we were both seniors, though she had attended APC for four years.

And that's all it took.

I was smitten.

I'm not sure why, but I just assumed that she was a pastor's daughter. She would later tell me that her dad was a farmer.

Not quite.

It took me about three weeks to find her again and ask her out. On our second date, New Year's Eve, 1974, I drove to her home in Santa Ana, fifty miles away. We went to dinner and saw a movie. As we drove down Fairview Avenue and passed Segerstrom Street, I asked, "Any relation?"

"It's named after my great-grandfather," she replied.

"Oh, interesting," I said. It should have tipped me off, but the information went right over my head.

When I met her parents, both seemed very welcoming and gracious. They had a lovely ranch-style house, not much different than the homes of my dad's bosses. Culturally, her parents seemed little different from my own. Her dad was a Mason, like my dad, wore a bolo tie, and drove a Buick. Both of her parents seemed very warm, also like my folks. No visible signs said anything other than that Susie Segerstrom had a normal family.

Susie and I graduated in May of 1975 and got engaged the following month. At that point, I became a regular weekend visitor to her parents' home, sleeping in the family room on the hide-a-bed. Every weekend, we had tacos on Saturday afternoon (her dad's favorite routine) and dinner at a nice restaurant. I enjoyed the restaurants, but they took me a while to get used to, as they were clearly out of my own family's routine. (I knew this because they placed more than one fork by my plate.) At the Hungry Tiger, the family's favorite restaurant, I had lobster tail for the first time, accompanied by a spinach salad with hot bacon dressing and stuffed mushrooms with crab. Such a menu vastly outclassed my own family's idea of a gourmet dinner, an annual visit to the Red Barn, where we'd order steak, eat it on a picnic table, and kick around sawdust on the floor.

As the Segerstroms welcomed me into their family, they also began to slowly reveal more of their financial holdings. Susie's great-grandfather, C. J. Segerstrom—the man for whom the street was named—had settled in the heart of Orange County in 1896. He started farming, and over the years the farm grew to more than twenty-two hundred acres. Life for the Segerstrom clan took a drastic change in 1965, when the 405 freeway was built to connect Los Angeles to San Diego. The freeway ran right through the middle of their farm, instantly making it prime real estate. They soon decided they might find a better use for the land than farming lima beans, so in 1966, they opened their first retail center, South Coast Plaza.

And that's when the truth suddenly hit me.

They're rich.

The revelation came as a total shock. I was not in any way prepared for it.

I knew how to live, quite happily, on very little. As a poor student, I had paid my way through college. But this curveball challenged me to my core, both psychologically and spiritually. As I pondered this unsettling new reality, I couldn't help but wonder what God was up to.

Was this some kind of Divine Comedy, borrowed from the Greek gods, who toy with their human subjects in order to get a laugh at their expense? This was certainly *not* how I foresaw my life unfolding! What about sacrificially serving God? I wasn't even remotely prepared to integrate a reality where wealth would be the rule rather than poverty. Try as I might, couldn't wrap my head around it.

Of course, Susie would never say, "We're rich." The word *rich* has become so stigmatized, in such negative ways, that she's never felt comfortable with it. I learned later that boys would not ask her out because they considered her out of their league. "She's too good for me," they'd say. I probably would have been one of them if I had known who she was when we started dating.

And so we began our lives together with a classic ignorance-is-bliss situation. My not knowing a thing about her family, or its financial potential, made it possible for us to date and to come to love each other, without this issue hanging over our heads to complicate things.

The complications, however, would come soon enough.

2

THE POVERTY GOSPEL

I grew up in the Lutheran church. So far as I can remember, none of my leaders ever taught that God wants us all to be healthy and wealthy. None of them, in other words, were fans of what's often called the prosperity gospel. On the other hand, I don't remember that they explicitly taught the opposite perspective, either.

Nevertheless, like too many in our society on both the left and the right of the theological spectrum, I held on to the idea that poverty *in and of itself* was more virtuous and brought people closer to God than did prosperity. If you had money, I reasoned, you gave it away. How else could you safeguard your soul? How else could you make sure you heard the longed-for words—"Well done, good and faithful servant. Enter into the joy of your Lord"—when you met Jesus at heaven's gate?

And so I proudly championed what I called "the poverty gospel."

A Corrupter of Souls?

Think back to all the messages you've heard regarding the temptations of material things.

If you grew up in a conservative church, you likely heard the implied message that wealth corrupts one's soul. Oh, it was never wrong to have *some* things in life, since our physical bodies require them, but you should *never* have luxurious things, and if you ever did get such things, certainly you should not enjoy them. Material wealth had a merely utilitarian purpose; anything more was borderline sinful. The wealthy lived in serious danger of allowing mere things to corrupt their souls.

In our more liberal churches, the wealthy still found themselves repeatedly censured, but for a very different reason. In these churches, people of capacity often got pictured as the greedy corrupters of society. The very fact that they had accumulated wealth provided evidence of their ungodliness. Almost certainly they had oppressed poor people to get it.

To this day, I still ask myself where I learned the underpinnings of such a faulty philosophy. Although my church never overtly said that money itself was the root of all evil, a subliminal message may have stowed away in the context of the church's preaching that conveyed that very notion. I never heard a single sermon or Sunday school lesson about the positive aspects of wealth. I don't recall hearing anything about Abraham using his wealth to bless others, or Joseph and Daniel rising to great spiritual heights even though both amassed large estates, or how a wealthy man—a courageous and godly follower—provided the tomb for Jesus's body after His crucifixion. I do remember a lot of negative lectures about riches, however, usually modeled after the story of the rich young ruler (see the next chapter).

Or maybe the message of the poverty gospel came to me from watching old movies about St. Francis of Assisi. Although

Francis grew up in a wealthy family, he turned from the comfort and privilege of wealth to embrace a life of godly service and poverty. St. Bonaventure, a Franciscan himself, wrote in his great thirteenth-century literary work *The Life of St. Francis* that Francis saw poverty as the surest path to God and assumed that "if we possess nothing, then nothing will get in the way of being possessed by Christ." The current pope models his life and style after the hallowed saint whose name he bears. I've always had enormous admiration for those who responded to a divine calling to make great personal sacrifices for the sake of others, modeled by our Lord Jesus Christ. As I watched those old films and read about St. Francis and others, I found myself, even as a young boy, moved deeply by what they did. I wished that I could do the same.

Wherever my perspective came from, I soon concluded that money itself was the root of all evil, even though the actual Bible verse says, "the *love of* money is *a* root of all *kinds of* evil" (1 Timothy 6:10, emphasis added). In my early Christian walk, I also assumed that to "deny myself, pick up the cross and follow Jesus" meant I had to choose the most difficult and burdensome path available. To put it more simply, I equated suffering with sacrificing for Jesus.

Whenever I had to make a choice about my direction in life, therefore, it became almost axiomatic that I had to choose the one that resulted in the greatest amount of suffering. How could I choose otherwise? For only in suffering could I become fully sacrificial.

In Bible school, I thought I might become a missionary. I wanted to follow in the footsteps of all those heroes of the faith whom I greatly admired—Hudson Taylor, Gladys Aylward, David Livingstone—brave men and women who gave up much to serve Christ. In the summer of 1973, I took a missionary trip to Nicaragua. I had told my dad that one of my main motivations for going was to suffer for my Lord by denying myself the luxuries of life for a summer of service. When I returned home, however, I said, "Dad, suffering isn't all it's cracked up to be."

With immutable wisdom, my father replied, "Son, you don't have to go looking for suffering in this world. It comes naturally."

But despite my dad's words, the exploits of famous missionaries and their sacrifices for Christ continued to enrapture me. When I read about Hudson Taylor and his wife Maria and the many hardships they endured, I could only think, *I want someone who can do that with me!* I hoped to find a wife who would want the same thing. Together, we would form a dynamic force for the kingdom of God!

On December 27, 1975, I married Susie, the love of my life. Only during our engagement period did her family begin to open the curtains on their true financial situation. Although their revelations gave me pause, her family members all seemed to be such natural, ordinary people that I never felt overwhelmed by their growing wealth. So far as I could see, we were all just regular people.

Although I never did hear God's call to go overseas, he did lead me to become a pastor. Susie joined me in Dubuque, Iowa, where three months before our marriage I had begun my seminary training at Wartburg Theological Seminary. After graduation, I knew, I could end up practically anywhere in the country. So far as I was concerned, as long as the family's business remained out of sight, it would stay out of mind.

Boy, was I wrong.

My first call brought me to a church in Orange County, where I would serve as an associate pastor in the very backyard of Susie's family business. That's when I first began to question, *Is there a purpose in all this?*

At seminary in faraway Iowa, I thought I would never have to deal with the complications of being rich. Now, back in Orange County, the complications stared at me everywhere. During those early years of marriage, I struggled tremendously with reconciling my "poverty is next to godliness" mentality with marrying into Susie's family. I couldn't help but feel that God was playing with me. I saw three possibilities at play:

A. This was a divine comedy.
B. God was teaching a self-righteous young man a thing or two.
C. God had a bigger purpose in it.

In hindsight, I realized I had stumbled into a fourth option:
D. All of the above.

Obedience Is Better Than Sacrifice

What did God want to teach me through all of this? Perhaps the words of the prophet Samuel best express it: "Obedience is better than sacrifice" (1 Samuel 15:22). God wanted me to live a life of obedience, where self-denial, sacrifice, and selflessness all become real.

Our goal should never be to pursue suffering, but to pursue God. If that pursuit brings suffering, so be it, but suffering itself is never to be our goal, no matter how noble and God honoring it may seem.

> *God wanted me to live a life of obedience,*
> *where self-denial, sacrifice, and selflessness*
> *all become real.*

Five years into my first pastorate, I had a chance to take a call to Salt Lake City. My sacrificial heart wept at the possibility that I could become Christ's ambassador in the heart of Utah. But the call never came. The call that did come would take me instead to a mission congregation in a comfortable suburban community in southern Orange County. Once again, God kept teaching me that it is better to obey Him than to strive to suffer for Him.

We sometimes mistakenly believe that Jesus went to the cross primarily to suffer for our sins, but what happened in the Garden of Gethsemane should change our minds. Three times, Jesus asked for the ultimate cup of suffering—the cross—to be removed from Him. More than anything, however, He wanted to do His Father's will. What drove Jesus to the cross was not a desire to suffer, but an unflinching passion to obey His Father's will.

To choose a sacrificial life does not mean to choose either

suffering or asceticism, but to seek whatever path God has laid before us so that we may do His will. If that choice leads to suffering, praise God. If that choice leads to a less painful path, praise God. Whether our choices lead to an impoverished life or to a life of great wealth, let us receive it with joy as those who have "set their faces like flint" to live in the will of God.

3

THE RICH YOUNG RULER

I f you were to randomly ask believers, "Which of Jesus's teachings best describes His view of wealth?" I'll bet that the majority, both lay and clergy, would reply, "The rich young ruler" (Mark 10:16–26). Although most Christians have memorized a limited number of Bible verses, I'm fairly certain that most of them could quote the words Jesus spoke to this man: "Go, sell all you have and give to the poor" (verse 21).

For a very long time, I lived under the naive assumption that Jesus meant to teach us that money has an inevitable way of burning a hole in a person's soul. Therefore, I thought, the best thing a rich person can do is get rid of the money, as quickly and expeditiously as possible. It never occurred to me that I might have missed Jesus's point altogether.

Unveiling a Personal Blind Spot

If the paradigm of the rich young ruler is the only one that governs how Christians of capacity should handle their resources, then the Gospel record should make that clear. As I pondered the story of the rich young ruler over the years, however, several unexpected observations began to dawn on me.

First, Jesus is recorded to have told only one person in all of Scripture to "sell all your goods and give to the poor." If He meant this command to apply to all wealthy Christians, then why didn't He give the same directive to more than one individual? I had no good answer to that question.

Second, to my greater surprise, Jesus had many wealthy friends and apparently never told *any* of them to sell all they had and give it to the poor. Jesus's own disciples Peter, James, and John owned their own fishing boats, and it takes capital to own a boat, both then and now. Several wealthy women often supported Jesus and His disciples out of their substantial resources (Luke 8:1), and not once did the Master order them to divest themselves of their riches. Three of Jesus's closest friends—Mary, Martha, and Lazarus—were wealthy, and He never told them to sell all they owned. In fact, He often enjoyed the comfort of their bigger-than-average house in Bethany. When Lazarus died of a sudden illness, Jesus returned to their home, not to reprimand them for holding on to their wealth, but to raise Lazarus from the dead—and by the way, only people of significant means owned their own tombs. Joseph of Arimathea, another wealthy convert to faith in Christ, laid Jesus in his own new tomb, freshly cut from the rock, after the crucifixion.

Everyone recognizes Jesus as a great teacher. His teaching gifts awe me, especially since my own seem miniscule by comparison. But if the Great Teacher had only one rule for His disciples of capacity—sell everything and give to the poor—then why didn't *any* of them get the message? It would seem that the requirement to sell everything one owns had specific application to the rich young ruler and had no regular place in Jesus's teaching.

Third, I ran into an existential problem with my interpretation of Jesus's words to the rich young ruler. I began to meet *many* devoted and responsible Christian people of capacity who appeared to handle their wealth in a godly manner. That blew my circuits, because it just didn't jibe with my long-held picture of the rich. Yes, these believers had wealth, but their attitudes and behavior seemed light-years removed from the rich young ruler.

So what was I to think? At the very least, my study of Scripture and my interactions with wealthy Christians had revealed a rather large blind spot in my understanding of faith and wealth.

A False Equation

I don't question the idea that money has an ability to foster tremendous dysfunction. It does. But by falsely equating wealth with materialism, I made several serious errors that caused me a lot of unnecessary anxiety and grief for too many years.

In fact, materialism is nothing more than defining yourself by what you own or desire to own. This means that the poor can be just as materialistic as the rich. You don't have to own something to be enslaved by it. The pursuit of riches, the thirst for material means, is enough to keep you in its bondage. So Jesus tells us, "Where your treasure is, there your heart will be also" (Matthew 6:21, NIV). Many of us keep our most cherished

treasures in thick vaults located nowhere but in our dreams—
and you don't need to own a thing to be consumed by such a
treasure. You need only to value that imaginary treasure above
all else.

When in 1 Timothy 6:17 the apostle Paul exhorts the rich not
to be arrogant or put their hope in wealth, he never adds, "By
the way, you should give it all away to the poor." I believe the
temptation that Paul saw confronting the wealthy in Timothy's
church mirrored the temptation that Jesus saw confronting the
rich young ruler. In both cases, wealth had become an ideal in
which some individuals had placed all their hope.

That's idolatry, plain and simple. And God will never let
idolatry go unchallenged.

Wealth, however, does not automatically equate with materialism. Justly earned wealth is as much a gift from God as
any of His other gifts (see chapter fifteen). Do we counsel those
who have the gift of mercy to beware using it too much, lest
they think of themselves as more loving than the Lord? Do we
warn those who have the gift of exhortation to minimize its use,
to avoid falling into the trap of intolerance? Not likely. On the
contrary, most churches regularly urge believers to use their
gifts liberally, wisely, and for God's glory.

Well, most gifts, anyway.

I see a great irony regarding the primary cure that many
churches offer for the very real temptation of money. Many
Christians of capacity sit in churches week after week, hearing
about the trials and temptations of wealth, only to hear the pastor say, "Give it to us." Is the church in the money-laundering
business? Can pastors and elders really can take that which is
impure in your hands and make it pure by putting it into theirs?

> *Wealth does not automatically equate with materialism. Justly earned wealth is as much a gift from God as any of His other gifts.*

In fact, when God's Spirit distributes His gifts, regardless of their nature, He expects the recipients to effectively use and steward those gifts. We glorify Him most, not when we attempt to escape from our God-given responsibility of stewardship, but when we strive to become the best stewards possible.

Twenty Years of Struggle

It took me twenty years of marriage to begin to understand all of this. During the first years of our marriage, I wanted to give away all of our wealth. I thought I was being noble and following the path of Christ. I often prayed that Christ would "take this cup from me" (although it really wasn't my cup to give, since it belonged to Susie).

Eventually I came to understand that my drive to be so "generous" had nothing to do with virtue. In fact, I had allowed fear to drive me. The responsibility to decide how to use this unexpected wealth frightened me.

A middle-class life, the kind I always thought I'd have, has a way of deciding for you how to spend your money. Most of your financial decisions concern how to provide for your family's daily needs and what portion to give to the Lord's work. A middle-class life, I thought, would have little left to tempt me.

But what happens when you suddenly have more—a *lot* more—than you need to live on? That scared me. I already felt haunted by questions I didn't feel ready to face. *How much do I need to give? What will it take for me to know that, at the judgment, Jesus will speak to me those wonderful words, "Well done, good and faithful servant"?*

After two decades of struggle, I learned we are to pursue only one standard, and that is God's unique leading for each of us. When Christ awakens within us a sense of our sinfulness, He tends to reveal piece by piece, step by step, throughout a lifetime, all that needs to come under His Lordship and grace.

The Bible does not intend for the story of the rich young ruler to be a universal principle that applies to every believer. Neither does it give us some cookie-cutter approach that lays out how each of us should live with the wealth God has given us. Though Christ calls each Christian to reflect His own amazing generosity, His Spirit leads each of us in unique ways.

He leads some to lives of poverty, either out of necessity for their own well-being (like the rich young ruler) or out of a sense of divine calling, which they receive with great joy. He asks others to steward their wealth in order to help fund the kingdom for years to come, or to maintain healthy businesses to provide for employees and their families. He leads some to do all their giving throughout their lifetime; others He directs to preserve capital for the next generation. Dietrich Bonhoeffer states it this way in his book *The Cost of Discipleship*: "It is not for us to choose which way we follow. That depends on the will of Christ."

While the journey differs for each of us (see chapter nineteen), the lifelong process remains the same. What areas of our lives have yet to come under God's rule and guidance? Or more positively, where in our lives do we still lack the joy that comes only through glad obedience?

4

THE PROBLEM OF IDENTITY

M y mom and dad came from a generation that believed you get your identity from what you do. And so for my first twenty-three years of life, I kept trying to find that thing that would define me. I started off wanting to build and race cars and then shifted to getting a job as a clerk at the FBI.

When I got my work badge—just an ID card with my picture on it and the letters *FBI* on top—I put it in my wallet next to my driver's license. That way, whenever I cashed a check, I would casually flash my card and all the clerks would say, "Oh, you work for the FBI."

I joined the FBI in part because I thought it would make me feel like somebody. My father loved telling people I worked for the FBI—but within a month, disillusionment set in. What I had pictured as an angelic organization turned out not to be so angelic. Contrary to what I'd seen on television, I spent some of my time retaking photos of agents who lost their IDs while getting drunk on a party boat, or working with other clerks who had chosen to shack up with one another. I heard that if you were ever in Washington, DC, and J. Edgar Hoover came walking down the hall, you should quickly find a broom closet to hide in. I worked at the FBI for only a year and a half, much to my dad's chagrin.

The Lord got hold of me during that time and I finally realized I could not find my worth in a job, but rather in the God who created me. I left for Bible School to prepare myself to become "a workman properly handling the word of truth" (see 2 Timothy 2:15). I assumed God intended to prepare me to go into the marketplace. I never considered becoming a pastor; I even brashly declared to God, "I will never be ordained."

The Pastorate and Beyond

By now, you know how my vow turned out. I became an ordained Lutheran pastor and served in that capacity for seventeen years.

When I left the pastorate to do foundation work, I didn't consider it a step backward or a step forward. It was simply a lateral move. Although being a pastor was never my identity, my wife and mom both asked me, "Well, if you're not a pastor, then who are you?"

When I resigned from my church, I often got asked, "Are you going to the bishop's office?" Many friends saw that as the next rung up the ladder of ministerial "success." I always felt tempted to answer, "God forbid, *no*." I'd learned as a young man working on the loading docks during college that I can serve God anywhere.

Although I felt ready to give up the pastorate and didn't need the title, I didn't want to give up my ordination quite yet. In the Lutheran church, you're not "once ordained, always ordained." So I took a three-year leave of absence and afterward had to requalify for ordination, either by doing interim church work or by accepting a call to a Lutheran hospital or school. The foundation work I'd begun wasn't a recognized form of call. The Community Church of Joy in Glendale, Arizona, told me, "If you ever need to hang out your shingle, you can hang it here," and I accepted the offer.

I agreed to help the church with stewardship issues and to work with its leadership center, training pastors. After five years of part-time service, I felt I had completed my work. During my exit interview with the bishop, I described my foundation work with Christians of capacity. He listened intently, congratulated me, wished me all the best, and then said the magic words: "You have a three-year leave of absence before you have to find another call." Wow! I was fifty-seven years old, would be sixty in three years, and could officially retire in my thirtieth year. I wouldn't have to worry about a call anymore. Nirvana!

These days, I spend most of my time with our family foundation, Sacred Harvest, without an organizational call. My work doesn't feel any less important to me than it ever has. I've always felt ministry is ministry, whether in the marketplace or in a foundation or anywhere else. I don't need a title to give me my identity. I feel complete and content in all that I'm doing. I feel whole.

But what if I couldn't do anything? What then?

The Idolatry of Usefulness

How would I view myself if ever lost my capacity to serve? Does my job or service define me? Many people have that problem. If they don't have a job or a place to serve, they wonder, *Who am I?* Sometimes I wonder if that is the biggest idolatry within the church today, the idolatry of our usefulness.

Let's say Susie somehow lost her money. Would that change who I am?

I have a friend who got his doctorate late in life. He told me that one of the things that got him started down that path was the thought, *It'd be cool to be called a doctor.* He called it a silly idea, but it did occur to him. After he became a PhD, the first few times people called him *Doctor,* he said it felt "weird." It didn't feel like "him." It didn't give him the feeling of satisfaction he thought it would.

While God created us to have purposeful lives, He never intended for us to find our worth and meaning through our purposefulness. He wants us to find our meaning in God Himself, from whom we are in Christ Jesus, quite apart from what we do or the titles we hold.

A time may come for each of us when our wealth disappears and we can no longer give as we do now. Or maybe our health fails and we no longer have the ability to remain physically active in ministry. When that day comes, will we still be able to see ourselves as valuable to God?

> *While God created us to have purposeful lives, He never intended for us to find our worth and meaning through our purposefulness. He wants us to find our meaning in God Himself.*

In Whose Hands Is Your Identity?

One of money's biggest problems is that it tempts the wealthy to find their self-esteem and self-worth from what they can hold in their hands, rather than from the One who holds them in His hands. In reality, Christians of capacity are no different than those who try to find their value and self-worth in their work or accomplishments.

We must never forget that whenever we define ourselves by anything other than that which is eternal, we end up defining ourselves by that which is temporal—things that can vanish or be taken away from us, long before we feel ready. And when we lose that part of us that gives us our identity, whether career, money, or home, we feel a great sense of worthlessness or even shame.

In doing so, we also injure our relationship with God by violating the first commandment ("You shall have no other gods before me"). A god is anything that gives us our identity and purpose in life. I know many wealthy individuals who suffer from a poverty of identity because they have never seen their wealth as a gift from God. They have allowed their wealth to become their identity… and such a god has a very short shelf life.

Be honest, now. Where do you find your own identity?

5

THE ROOT OF ALL EVIL

O ne of the saddest things about many of our favorite movie lines is that they don't actually exist.

Casual fans of *Dirty Harry* love to quote the line "Do you feel lucky, punk?" Except that no one in the movie ever said it. The line really goes, "You've got to ask yourself one question, 'Do I feel lucky?' Well, do ya, punk?"

Or how about the famous line from *Casablanca*, "Play it again, Sam"? In fact, the quotation is, "You played it for her, you can play it for me. If she can stand it, I can. Play it!"

When we quote such lines from memory, very often we get them wrong. We shorten them, substitute or transpose words, put the emphasis on a different part of the sentence—and the false line takes on a life of its own. No, Darth Vader never actually said, "Luke, I am your father." Sorry! He said instead, "No. I am your father."

Fortunately, we do little harm when we misquote these lines. And sometimes, the misquotations actually improve the originals. Which is better: "Badges? We don't need no stinkin' badges!" or "Badges? We ain't got no badges. We don't need no badges. I don't have to show you no stinkin' badges!" (from *The Treasure of the Sierra Madre*)?

Unfortunately, however, we also misquote famous Bible verses—and the result is never an upgrade. That's especially true of 1 Timothy 6:10.

A Harmful Change

How often have you heard the line "Money is the root of all evil"? I used to think about it incessantly. And I sincerely believed it! I thought the apostle Paul wholeheartedly agreed with me in supposing that the *only* godly thing to do with money was to give it away. How could you hang on to pure evil, something that would always turn your heart into a stone as cold and black as night?

Except that the good apostle never wrote that line. Here's the full quotation, with the misquoted portion in italics:

> People who want to get rich fall into temptation and a trap and into many foolish and harmful desires that plunge men into ruin and destruction. *For the love of money is a root of all kinds of evil.* Some people, eager for money, have wandered from the faith and pierced themselves with many griefs. (1 Timothy 6:9–10)

Did you notice the difference? The oft-quoted version says, "Money is the root of all evil." The actual quote reads, "the *love of* money is *a* root of *all kinds of* evil." Unlike many gaffes in quoted movie lines, this change—the dropping of "love of" being the biggest—materially changes the sense of the quotation. It goes from being a wise and necessary warning against placing your hope, trust, and confidence in money to becoming a condemnation of money itself.

Mark Twain might say that's the difference between lightning and the lightning bug. Lightning bugs are kind of cute. Lightning can kill you.

I don't want to downplay Paul's warning about the dangers of improperly handling money, because those dangers are both real and serious. Those who make the acquisition of wealth the chief goal of their lives *do* wander from the faith and they *do* pierce themselves with many griefs and they *do* plunge to their own ruin and destruction. Idolatry always kills, and Paul clearly calls greed "idolatry" (Colossians 3:5). When we set our hearts on accumulating money, our minds very naturally focus on "earthly things," our "god" becomes our "stomach" and our "glory" becomes our "shame," which makes us into "enemies of Christ" (see Philippians 3:18–19).

The truth is that wealth is a deeply spiritual matter—which is why God talked so much about it long before Paul ever came on the scene.

Show Restraint

Although for many years I misinterpreted the story of the rich young ruler, Jesus did use the encounter to tell His disciples,

"How hard it is for the rich to enter the kingdom of God!" (Mark 10:23). Why would He say such a thing? He said it because unless the wealthy come to understand their riches as a gift from God, given to them to use to bless others and glorify God, they can easily move to hoarding it for themselves and putting their hope and trust in it.

No doubt Jesus had a host of Old Testament texts in mind as He spoke about the rich young ruler. Consider just a few.

> Do not wear yourself out to get rich; have the wisdom to show restraint. (Proverbs 23:4)

> Though your riches increase, do not set your heart on them. (Psalm 62:10)

> Whoever trusts in his riches will fall. (Proverbs 11:28)

> Hoarding riches harms the saver. (Ecclesiastes 5:13, NLT)

> A faithful man will be richly blessed, but one eager to get rich will not go unpunished. (Proverbs 28:20)

Without question, wealth is a spiritual matter. Christians of capacity face temptations and challenges that others don't. *And yet*, money itself is not the problem. People misuse sex, too, but sex isn't the problem. The problem lies not in the thing itself, but in the hearts of those who use the thing.

Money Is a Magnifier

Some like to say that money is neutral, that everything depends on how one uses it. I prefer to say that money is not neutral, but it is a magnifier. Money simply magnifies who we really are.

Fame or celebrity status, like wealth, also magnifies what a person is on the inside. When we look at the lives of great actors such as Tom Hanks and Denzel Washington, we see people whose fame did not corrupt their virtue; in fact, it has helped to make it more apparent. But we can all think of many others for whom fame served only to magnify their licentious, self-centered living, and so reveal the foolishness in their hearts.

> *Money is not neutral, but it is a magnifier. Money simply magnifies who we really are.*

The same is true with wealth. If selfish, foolish individuals acquire great wealth, what do they become? They don't become more generous; they just become bigger fools. But those who have learned to be generous and noble with little usually become even more generous and noble with much (see Luke 16:10–11).

This is the challenge given to Christians of capacity. Will we be like the faithful stewards in the parable of the talents, to whom the king (God) entrusts a portion of His own wealth, expecting them to strive to fulfill God's purposes of blessing Him, their families, their neighbors, and their church? God is not, as many have tried to describe Him, an ascetic who believes that wealth and material things are evil in and of themselves and thus must be avoided or minimized. But neither is He a materialist who believes that wealth, in and of itself, is naturally good. In fact, wealth is a magnifier, revealing what exists in the hearts of those who (temporarily) have it.

God teaches us that wealth can be a very good thing, even a very spiritual thing. When used properly, it can draw us closer to Him. But when misused, it can become a force that either weakens faith or, most disastrous of all, becomes the object of faith. Wealth itself doesn't make someone holy or hellish, wise or foolish, generous or stingy, loving or hateful. Wealth is a magnifier that merely reveals what already exists in a person's heart.

Don't Look for a Formula

In the past, I fell into the trap that so many others continue to struggle with today: Should we Christians of capacity take a minimalist view or a maximalist view of our livelihood? While I am definitely not into the prosperity gospel, I believe that the other extreme can become just as troubling. "Keep only the bare minimum for yourself!" is no better a formula for living than is "Keep it all for yourself!"—especially if either is viewed as the *only* formula for life.

Poverty is not next to godliness, any more than conspicuous consumption is a sign of God's blessing. I would never contest either the devotion or choice of those today who endorse the mantra "live simply that others may simply live." But I also would never agree that it's a one-size-fits-all formula for living, or even that it means the same thing for everyone.

An idol is nothing more than that in which we find our identity and purpose and in which we place our hope, rather than in God. Slogans can become idols, too. Yes, wealth carries great temptations, even perilous ones. But Scripture never equates money, in and of itself, with the root of all evil. Only in the *love* and *pursuit* of money—wealth for the sake of our own self-importance—can riches ensnare us and turn our hearts from our greatest good and love.

6

JUDGING THE WEALTHY

A fter the Lord got hold of my heart in the early '70s and I left my job at the FBI, I sold the very thing that so often had defined my existence: my car.

I was sold out to God!

Although I had never been a tither prior to that time, once I became convinced that God's Word says a faithful follower of God tithes, I didn't see how I could do anything less. At Bible school, I sat down after every week's payday to figure out where to send my 10 percent. Out of my fifty bucks a week, I felt proud that I could give five dollars to the causes for Christ that I loved. Though I paid rent (fifty dollars each month netted me a room in a grand old house), Bible school cost me $125 each quarter, and I needed money for food, I always believed that I had more than enough.

But while God had given me a most cheerful attitude about tithing, I cannot say I had an equally positive attitude toward people of financial means. *Real* Christians, it seemed to me, had to live frugally and sacrificially. I believed that God wanted me—which is to say, *all* committed followers of Jesus—to live just above the poverty level. Any lifestyle not characteristic of these traits was clearly materialistic.

One day I got together for lunch with a dear Christian friend who had just started his career as a CPA. Since I was now the poor Bible school student, he offered to pay for my meal. No problem for me! But then he pulled out a *credit card* to pay.

I can still recall the shock I felt when I saw him produce this icon of materialism (remember, this took place when Master-Card and Visa were just getting launched). I felt aghast that a Christian would ever use one, let alone *own* one. (Don't look at my wallet today!)

And as if that weren't enough, when we walked to the parking lot and I headed toward my ten-year-old Pontiac Tempest, I watched him get into a brand-new Audi 5000. As I said good bye to my friend, with whom I had prayed and studied the Scriptures for almost two years, I left with a sense of self-righteous arrogance that could only belittle him in my eyes.

Where there is money, I thought, *there can only be the love of money.*

Forget that his faith prompted him to tithe! Forget that his commitment to Christ helped him to live faithfully to his Lord! If he refused to give up all his money, then he was walking in contempt of God, just like the rich young ruler.

That perfectly summarized my theology at the time.

Nothing but Contempt

I share this story as an embarrassing confession, not as one who had really discovered the right and true way. I tell you about it not as one who had become more righteous and godly than his friend, but as an immature believer who as yet couldn't even conceive of the challenging contours of the trip ahead.

My attitude merely manifested my own self-righteousness. I had employed my own version of reverse discrimination, without even recognizing what I had done. Like so many other Christians, I felt nothing but contempt for those followers of Jesus who had received more material blessings than I had. I saw myself as just a "little bit more equal than they" in the eyes of God.

I was among the chosen; they were among the fallen.

They had bowed the knee to the great god Mammon; I had remained faithful to Jesus.

While they had chosen the path of selfishness, I had chosen the path of sacrifice.

While they would ruin their lives on the rocky shoals of money, I would sail confidently into the safe harbor of God's grace, where money counts for nothing.

I felt as if my friend had thrown his credit card in my face. So of course, I would throw stones at him for his lack of spiritual sense. And I got pretty good at it, too.

We Attack What We Don't Know

We tend to cast stones at what we don't know. Can you guess the biggest reason why I had such a self-righteous attitude toward wealthy people?

It really isn't all that complicated—I didn't *know* any wealthy people.

I'd never heard anything but negative stories about them. No one had ever shown me any positive examples of godly men and women using their wealth in ways that glorified God and blessed others. And since I saw only negative examples, I thought only negative thoughts.

I therefore kept a bag of stones at my side, in easy reach, ready to cast a few whenever the occasion arose. And this made me feel *very* good about myself.

But my whole worldview started taking a beating once I met some friends of Susie's mom and dad, who took the stewardship of their resources seriously and responsibly. I watched them provide sound financial leadership in their communities in a way that—*gasp!*—didn't fit at all with the money-grubbing paradigm I had cherished for so long.

> *While people tend to brag about their résumé virtues—what they've done, who they know— what gets remembered long after they're gone are their eulogy virtues.*

From a biblical perspective, can you be a good steward without having faith? The answer is, "Yes, to a degree." Susie's parents had modeled one aspect of stewardship, generosity, but it never became an act of worship for them. In their stewardship, they gave back to their community from which they had greatly benefited. They did so without grandstanding and they gave without thought of how it might benefit them in the long run.

When Hal, Susie's dad, passed away, I asked in my funeral sermon, "How do you measure a person's life? Is it by your success, by your notoriety, by your Dun and Bradstreet? If that's the case, then Hal had it all. But those who knew him well measured Hal's life by his kindness, by his charity, by his concern, by his friendship."

David Brooks, author of the *New York Times* best-seller *The Road to Character*, makes a helpful distinction between résumé virtues and eulogy virtues. While people tend to brag about their résumé virtues—what they've done, who they know—what gets remembered long after they're gone are their eulogy virtues. Hal had the latter, in spades.

So are the one percenters among us *really* the ones who cause most of the world's problems, as so many seem to think today? A large part of our society believes that if you're wealthy, then you must have earned it in an unrighteous manner. You must have gained it by leeching off the sweat and blood of others.

Do you know of any *positive* connotations for the word *rich*? When the word gets used to describe someone, it usually carries a negative tone. What believer walks around saying, "I'm rich"? Susie and I don't. Instead I like to say, "I'm a Christian of capacity," or "We're believers of means." And if in some conversation you do mention it, very likely you'll be perceived as bragging. Christians of modest means will think you're saying you're better than they are.

But what would happen if you were to walk up to the

same individuals and say, "May I give you a check for a million dollars"? How many would say, "No, thanks"? Much less than one out of a million, I'd wager.

Pocketing the Stones

Judgment comes easy regarding those rich people "out there," those oppressors of the poor who gained their wealth through subjugation, theft, or worse! Before I started meeting some rich people, I had never seriously considered what the whole Bible says about the wealthy. Yes, I knew that Jesus once said, "Woe to you who are rich, for you have already received your comfort" (Luke 6:24), but I had never stopped to contemplate what it might mean when the Scripture also said things like, "The LORD makes some poor and others rich" (1 Samuel 2:7, NLT).

If the Lord made some rich—godly men like Abraham, Boaz, David, and others—then who was I to cast stones at them?

I actually rather liked it when I heard James thunder, "Now listen, you rich people, weep and wail because of the misery that is coming upon you. Your wealth has rotted, and moths have eaten your clothes. Your gold and silver are corroded. Their corrosion will testify against you and eat your flesh like fire" (James 5:1–3). But I never bothered to notice that James directed his scathing rebukes not to "rich people" in general, but to those who had "hoarded wealth," to those who had "failed to pay the workmen who mowed your fields," to those who had "lived on earth in luxury and self-indulgence" and

43

who "condemned and murdered innocent men, who were not opposing you." Such men had "fattened" themselves for "the day of slaughter," James predicted (verses 3–6). Hooray!

But what was I to do with a God who would say to a band of ancient Christians, "You will be made rich in every way so that you can be generous on every occasion, and through us your generosity will result in thanksgiving to God" (2 Corinthians 9:11)?

I really didn't know. But unknown to me, I would soon find out.

7

THE WIDOW'S MITE

While Jesus spoke a great deal about money and its rightful place in our lives, He also made it a point to observe what men and women did with their money. Probably the most famous example of the latter is the story of the widow's mite:

> Jesus sat down opposite the place where the offerings were put and watched the crowd putting their money into the temple treasury. Many rich people threw in large amounts. But a poor widow came and put in two very small copper coins, worth only a fraction of a penny. Calling His disciples to Him, Jesus said, "I tell you the truth, this poor widow has put more into the treasury than all the others. They all gave out of their wealth; but she, out of her poverty, put in everything—all she had to live on." (Mark 12:41–44)

We know this story by the name "the widow's mite" because the King James Version of the Bible identified the two "very small copper coins" as "mites." In fact, these were leptons, the smallest coin minted in the ancient Greek world. In Jesus's day, a lepton equaled 1/128 of a denarius, worth about a day's wages. So this poor widow contributed 1/64 of a day's wages to the temple treasury. By way of comparison, suppose for a moment that they had minimum wage laws in those days (they didn't), and further suppose for simplicity's sake that the minimum wage was set at ten dollars an hour. A person working a full day at that rate, then, would earn eighty dollars. Take 1/64th of that number, and we could say the widow put in about five quarters… and her tiny gift just wiped her out. She had nothing more. No more quarters. No dimes, no nickels, not even a penny. She gave to God everything she had.

> *If you knew you were about to die, would you spend a chunk of your time watching how people gave away their money?*

As I read the story, several questions occur to me:
- *How could Jesus tell the denomination of the coins?* Apparently, He had to be sitting fairly close by. He *wanted* to see.
- *How did Jesus know the woman had no more money?* Just like He knew so many other "secret" things about a person's private, personal life, I guess (see John 4:17–18; Matthew 9:4; Luke 6:8).
- *How often did Jesus watch people put money into the temple treasury?* I don't know, but it doesn't appear that

He did so at this occasion on a whim. It looks very deliberate. He seems to have stayed there for some time, just watching.

- *Why did Jesus pick this activity as His last public act before His arrest and crucifixion?* Again, I don't know, but I find the fact very interesting. And maybe a little troubling. If you knew you were about to die, would you spend a chunk of your time watching how people gave away their money?

- *Why did Jesus say that the woman put in "more" than everyone else, even those who contributed "large amounts"?* Maybe He was going by percentages—100 percent is certainly larger than 1 percent. Or maybe He used some other calculation, such as size of hope (or desperation)?

- *Why didn't Jesus commend anyone else?* Jesus watched a lot of people contribute to the temple fund that day, but He commended only one poor woman. Why? I'm not sure. Do we have to give away all we have in order to receive a divine commendation? I doubt we have to assume that God dismissed everyone else's contribution that day as insignificant. Jesus didn't mean to start an offering war; but He did want to make a very important point to His disciples. But what was that point, exactly?

- *What happened to the woman afterward?* If Jesus knew the widow had just given her last penny, then how did God reward her faith? We're not told. If we had been told, I imagine we'd find some way to skew the meaning of the story. We're all on a walk of faith; none of us learns the end of our stories before they end.

While I still wonder all these things, I now wonder if I have my questions all wrong. What if the story is not so much about the amazing faith of the widow as it is about the odious greed of the scribes? Immediately before Mark tells us this story, he reports Jesus's caustic words about the "teachers of the law. They like to walk around in flowing robes and be greeted in the marketplaces, and have the most important seats in the synagogues and the places of honor at banquets. *They devour widows' houses* and for a show make lengthy prayers. Such men will be punished most severely" (Mark 12:38–40, italics added).

Did Jesus point out the widow's contribution to emphasize His earlier lesson about the diabolical greed of the religious leaders? Was she exhibit A in the category of "widows' houses consumed by religious covetousness"?

I don't know. Maybe.

I do know that, unlike the widow who gave all she had as an act of worship and faith in her God (and perhaps out of fear of what the religious leaders might do to her if she didn't?), the Pharisees made their offerings to honor themselves by giving in ways that trumpeted their own generosity. It is said that thirteen large chests with trumpetlike openings were scattered around the temple compound in Jesus's day, in which worshippers could place their contributions. Those who wanted to call attention to their gifts brought the largest number of coins possible, so that when they threw their offerings into the chests, no one could ignore the noise the coins made.

Second, while the widow gave because she wanted to, the Pharisees gave only because they had to in order to keep up their public image. Therefore, while the widow gave far more than what the law mandated, the Pharisees gave no more than required (their tithe). Even though they tithed from everything they owned—"their mint, rue, and all other kinds of garden herbs" (Luke 11:42)—they were nothing more than bean counters who wanted merely to satisfy the minimal requirement of the law. This would excuse them (so they imagined) from having to embrace the whole spirit of the law. By scrupulously holding to the letter of the law, they ended up neglecting justice and the love of God (see Matthew 23:23).

This reminds me that whenever someone imposes the law upon us to give, even when that law is "you must tithe to the church," we often go the Pharisees' route. Consider the stark differences between mandatory and voluntary giving:

	Have to Give	Want to Give
How willing is the giver?	Reluctant	Eager
How great is their effort?	Minimum	Maximum
What is the effect on the giver?	Regret	Joy
What is the impact on the recipient?	Ambivalence	Gratitude

When I think of the greatest example of giving in the Old Testament, I don't think about tithes at all, but about a "free-will offering" recorded in Exodus 35–36. The Lord instructed

Moses to take an offering designed to fund the building of the tabernacle, inviting "everyone who is willing" (35:5) and "whose heart moved him" (verse 21, also verses 22, 26, 29) to give. Boy, did they ever! Morning after morning they gave, until the skilled craftsmen assigned to do the work finally had to wave their hands and—with laughter on their faces—say, "Stop! Stop!"

They told Moses, "The people are bringing more than enough for doing the work the LORD commanded to be done." Even when Moses directed the people to stop bringing their offerings, they had to be "restrained from bringing more" (36:5–6).

Restrained from giving? You have to love it!

So then, which of the two giving styles listed above elicits eager, maximum, joyful, and thankful gifts?

Or I think of the longest passage focused on giving anywhere in the Bible. In 2 Corinthians 8–9, Paul describes the financially poor believers in Macedonia, whose "overflowing joy and their extreme poverty welled up in rich generosity. For I testify that they gave as much as they were able, and even beyond their ability. Entirely on their own, they urgently pleaded with us for the privilege of sharing" their few resources with the stricken believers in Jerusalem, people they didn't even know who lived hundreds of miles away (2 Corinthians 8:2–4). In the rest of the passage, Paul repeatedly uses words like *desire* and *eager willingness* and *enthusiasm* and *thanksgiving* and *generosity* to describe the kind of giving that most pleases God, all of it fueled by "grace" (a term used ten times in the Greek original).

Again, which list above describes giving in terms like "eager," "maximum," "joyful," and "thankful"?

What Does It Mean?

So what does the story of the widow's mite *mean*? Are we to give away all that we have? Maybe some of us should. Are we to use her example of sacrificial giving to inform and motivate our own giving? No doubt. Are we to take special care that we don't become like these ancient teachers of the law, greedy men who devoured widows' homes to fuel their own lifestyles? Certainly I don't want to be a relativist when it comes to interpreting Scripture, but perhaps in this case, the best question to ask is this: *What does this story mean to you?*

8

STEALTH BOMBER

D uring the majority of our years in the pastorate, Susie drove minivans while I drove an SUV. We saw this lifestyle choice as an important way to fit in with our community. At the same time, however—unknown to most members of our church—we secretly stashed away in our garage a Stealth Bomber.

The Orange County performing arts center had opened in 1986, on land donated by Susie's family. In honor of their contribution, the concert hall was named Segerstrom Hall. (About four years ago, the name of the whole center changed to the Segerstrom Center for the Arts.) We had three or four black-tie events to attend each year, and while Susie loved her Astro van and I loved my Chevy Blazer, I didn't think we should show up for them in a van or a truck. That's when we bought our "going out on the town" car, a black Mercedes, aka Stealth Bomber.

Could we afford it? Absolutely. We wrote out a check at the beginning of a recession and bought the car in a cash deal. No doubt many who saw a new Mercedes driving around town thought, *Oh, boy, sucker! He's going to get stuck.* I felt almost like putting a license plate frame on the car that said, "Don't laugh, it's paid for."

Did the car cause us to compromise our giving in any way? Absolutely not. Nevertheless, that car never once darkened the church's parking lot.

We've heard similar stories from others. Our pastor's wife tells how her aunt, married to a pastor, secretly hid her nice china and collectibles whenever members of the church came to their home for a visit.

Why all this need for stealth bombers and hidden china? I can think of at least three reasons.

Stealth Christians

What prompts Christians of capacity to go into stealth mode? Why do they often hide their wealth from other Christians?

First, many Christians of capacity simply *don't want to be judged.*

As a pastor, I didn't want to appear as though we were flaunting our possessions. All too often, the church makes the wealthy feel self-conscious about what they have, to the point that they try to hide their gift of resources from their brothers and sisters in Christ.

When someone stands out in a crowd, he often gets labeled as "better than thou," sometimes out of jealousy or envy. In Australia, I'm told, average Aussies like to say that "tall poppies get cut down." A "king of the hill" mentality can prompt people to say things like, "She thinks she's better than everybody else, just because she has money." Who wants that? It's easier just to hide.

Before I met Susie, I think I would have been in this crowd.

I probably would have belittled whatever wealthy Christians did for others, or at least called their motives into question.

While some of the people in the churches we served knew something of our wealth, it never became a problem for us, probably because of our generosity. Generally speaking, if people know and understand that you're generous, it's pretty hard for them to throw stones at you. Not impossible, but harder.

Second, Christians of capacity *don't want to be viewed as being different from everyone else.*

Even now, Susie sometimes downplays her wealth when she doesn't want to be perceived as different. When she talks about her past, for example, she often says things like, "We didn't have much. I'm no different from you. We have a shared experience."

In recent conversations with our children, Jenny and Matt, I found out that even in elementary school, our children got teased because they were Segerstroms—and they didn't even carry the name. Word got around anyway.

> *Hard experience has caused many Christians of capacity to become suspicious of other people's motives in wanting to get to know them.*

I used to wonder why Jenny seldom brought friends to the house. Even when she went off to college, she brought no one home for a visit until late in her junior year. Understand that the friends of our children almost always came from families who had to work hard just to get by. I suppose Jenny and Matt felt most comfortable with them, because that describes most of *our* friends. I think Jenny worried that her friends would perceive her as "showing off" if they were to see our home.

Our wealth also has led us to a predicament we've had to learn how to navigate. When we go on a trip with friends, we often find ourselves scaling down what we want to do so that they can afford it, or we have to subsidize them up to the level we want. In everyday living, of course, we generally behave and live like most average people. The only big difference is the way we try to model our giving.

Third, hard experience has caused many Christians of capacity to become suspicious of other people's motives in wanting to get to know them.

Susie's dad was a prime example of someone who didn't really know who his friends were. In the last ten years of his life, when the family business really began to prosper, he grew suspicious of new relationships because people always seemed to want something from him. You really can start feeling used after a while.

Strangers occasionally call me and immediately start trying to create a best friend relationship. One guy, every inch the salesman, very assured of himself, friendly and warm, said he wanted to start a ministry. He wanted to get together in the near future.

"Hey, how about if I take you to lunch next week?" he said. "I belong to the club here. We'll get our wives together, too." He was trying to force the relationship down a certain path. I never called him—he always called me.

After one call, a couple of months would go by and then I'd get another call. "Hey, let's get together for lunch." Just like old buds!

Eventually I started coaching him about setting up a non-profit. "I need to raise such-and-such kind of money," he explained.

When I asked him, "What's your budget?" he replied, "I'm thinking about $300,000 a year."

I then asked him my test question to ferret out his true motivation: "Are you taking anything for a salary?"

"Yeah, I need to get $150,000 a year," he answered. As soon as the words came out of his mouth, I knew he merely wanted to create a nice paycheck for himself.

Some friends who really want to raise money for this or that organization see us only as "cows to be milked," a colorful phrase used by my friend Howard Ahmanson. When you milk a cow, she is not necessarily willing to give it to you; you take it from her. I have a degree of tolerance with such individuals, until it becomes obvious what they're really about.

Some people in the larger Christian community also try to communicate friendship in ways that appear disingenuous. Fortunately, I have a good BS meter that can smell it right away.

No Longer Hiding

Susie and I have lived with wealth for long enough now that we don't really try to hide it much anymore. Our Stealth Bomber came out of the closet years ago. I hope that what Paul said two millennia ago we can say today: "What we are is plain to God, and I hope it is also plain to your conscience" (2 Corinthians 5:11).

Still, there are those times. There will be for you, too. Better to know they're coming than to get surprised by them!

9

SCHINDLER'S CURSE

The 1993 movie *Schindler's List* won seven Academy Awards, set box office records for a black-and-white film, and regularly gets included among history's top motion pictures. The film, based on the 1982 novel *Schindler's Ark*, chronicles how an ethnic German industrialist named Oskar Schindler went from war profiteer and Nazi party member to savior of about twelve hundred Jews who otherwise would have perished in the Holocaust. By the end of World War II, Schindler had spent his entire fortune, primarily through bribes, to keep his Jewish factory workers alive.

A scene at the end of the movie shows Schindler leaving his factory at night, surrounded by the grateful men and women whose lives he had managed to spare. He is given a gold ring inscribed in Hebrew with words from the Talmud: "He who saves one life saves the world entire." Schindler, his voice breaking and body trembling, replies, "I could have got more out. ...I could have got more. ...*I didn't do enough.*"

It's a beautiful, ugly, haunting, and inspiring scene, just like the rest of the film. And it focuses for me a sharp dilemma that I've felt for a long time, although in a far less dramatic fashion. That scene powerfully highlights a question that has troubled me ever since I learned that Susie and I would not have a middle-class life but one of abundance. Yes, we have always given generously to worthy causes around the world—but how much is enough? Couldn't we do even more? Couldn't we keep less for ourselves and give more to others?

That's Schindler's curse, and it's haunted me for decades.

A Growing Struggle

Just before Susie and I got married and went off to seminary, her grandfather pulled me aside and gave me a check for $3,000. "This is to help you get your nest egg going," he said. No one in my entire life had ever given me such a large gift. With part of the money, I bought us a new bed (what else would a newly-wed buy?) and we rented all our other furniture. For three years, we lived quite happily in a fourteen-by-seventy-foot mobile home.

After I graduated, we returned to California, where I served for five years in a wonderful Huntington Beach church. We still didn't have a tremendous amount of money, although by then Susie had perhaps $30,000 in the bank. Her grandmother gave us a loan so we could buy our first house, at 6 percent interest.

About six years into my next pastorate in Laguna Niguel, Susie's income distribution from her family's investments started to rise. The family business continued to expand, adding office buildings and other income-generating properties, which probably made us the richest people in the church, at least in terms of assets.

From then on, living with wealth caused me intense and growing struggles. If I didn't give it all away (even though, again, it really wasn't mine to give), then did that mean I'd sold out to a materialistic worldview? Surely, we could have done more for underprivileged men and women had we chosen to live on just 5 percent less. But then, couldn't we do even more on 8 percent less? Twelve percent less? Fifty percent? Seventy?

I remember one year when our taxes exceeded our quarterly distributions. By then, we were giving away a quarter of our income. *Wait a second,* I thought, *if we give our 25 percent out of that now, we'll have to dip into our savings to pay our taxes.* So I tried to create a mathematical equation to determine how much to give that would equal 25 percent. I played with that algorithm for months, to no avail. After all those weeks of fruitless computation, I began to realize how silly it was... but I still didn't have an answer.

How much is enough? Couldn't we give more than we do? As our income continued to climb throughout our first fifteen years of marriage, Schindler's curse haunted me more every day.

Finding Balance

Would have, could have, should have.

Once you let it start, it never ends.

Did I *really* need that new set of golf clubs? Did I *really* need that new car? Couldn't I have used that money to teach a poor Filipino boy to read?

John Calvin has a passage in *The Institutes* where he discusses this very question: How much should we keep for ourselves of the material things God has given us to steward? If I give away a pair of shoes, I still have a linen shirt. Should I give away the linen shirt and wear a hair shirt instead? But then I'd still have a hair shirt. Should I give that away and use a potato sack instead?

Where does it stop?

How do we find a godly balance between being generous and enjoying what God has given to us? What *does* God require of us? When you search the Bible, you find a bit of a mixed bag. For example:

- John the Baptist told God's people to "produce fruit in keeping with repentance" and counseled them that, "The man with two tunics should share with him who has none, and the one who has food should do the same" (Luke 3:11).
- 1 Timothy 6:17 insists that God "richly provides us with everything for our enjoyment."
- Jesus sometimes walked away from needy crowds (Matthew 13:58).
- 1 Timothy 5:8 warns us that a person who does not provide for his family is worse than an unbeliever.
- Jesus angered His hometown neighbors by reminding them that God didn't heal everybody or bring everybody relief from famine (Luke 4:25–27).
- John asked, "If anyone has material possessions and sees his brother in need but has no pity on him, how can the love of God be in him?" (1 John 3:17).

It would seem that although Christ wants us to develop a spirit of generosity, He does not give us a set of boxes to check off: "Did this, did this, this, this, this. I'm good." Law gives you parameters. Grace does not. The problem with grace is that you never know if you're meeting your quotas. How do you figure out how much is enough? It's hard to hit the tape when it feels like the finish line is on roller skates and keeps moving away the closer you get. At least with a formula, you know if you hit the mark.

With grace, *is* there a quota?

Would it have helped me, do you suppose, if God had recorded for us Abraham's annual income in Scripture? Suppose we knew how much he kept for himself and how much he gave away. Do you think that would become a law?

Without question, it would become a law. We would have made it into the Abraham box. We want benchmarks so we know when we're done. If it's 50 percent that God wants from me, or 60 percent or 70 percent, then I know the rest is mine and I can do with it whatever I want... can't I?

> *I believe God wants to create in us a spirit of stewardship, not a law of stewardship. We please Him most, not by hitting some precise percentage, but by exercising our faith in a gracious God.*

The End of the Curse

How do we live by a spirit of grace that brings freedom and joy without compromising our responsibility? How do we respond to God's grace in faith?

When it comes to money, many of us want a law, a hard-and-fast rule, a definitive percentage. We want to find the truth in the very letters themselves and not in the spirit of what God says to us. A member of my first church read Psalm 90:10—"The length of our days is seventy years—or eighty, if we have the strength"—in a strictly literal way. This man believed God *guaranteed* a righteous person at least seventy years. I thought, *But what about Jesus?* Our Lord didn't even make it to half of that number! But the man just couldn't give up on his belief, regardless of the evidence.

Paul tells us that God "has made us competent as ministers of a new covenant—not of the letter but of the Spirit; for the letter kills, but the Spirit gives life" (2 Corinthians 3:6). I believe God wants to create in us a spirit of stewardship, not a law of stewardship. We please Him most, not by hitting some precise percentage, but by exercising our faith in a gracious God.

When at the end of the movie Oskar Schindler whispers that he didn't do enough, his Jewish friend and former employee answers, "You did so much." In fact, more than seven thousand descendants of "Schindler's Jews" are alive today because of what he did. After his death in 1974, Schindler was buried in Jerusalem on Mount Zion, the only member of the Nazi Party ever so honored.

"When someone has been given much," Jesus said, "much will be required in return" (Luke 12:48, NLT). What is your "much"? I can't say. I have a hard enough time determining my own "much"! But I do know that, whatever it is, when you give it in faith and not by mere formula, it always breaks the power of Schindler's curse.

10

A NOTE FROM MILLARD FULLER

A s we rolled into 1995, Susie's family business continued to grow and our income expanded like never before, making us one of the wealthiest families in the church I pastored. I definitely had not seen *that* coming.

And that's when the issue of money *really* became a hot potato for me.

What were we supposed to do with all of it? We faithfully gave our tithes and offerings to kingdom causes, but so much remained! I just didn't know which way to turn.

One day as I pondered all of this, I picked up Millard Fuller's 1994 book, *The Theology of the Hammer*. The book tells his story—and quite a story it is. I resonated with it immediately.

Giving It All Away

Fuller grew up in humble surroundings in Alabama, graduated from Auburn University and then from law school at the University of Alabama. He and a college friend began a marketing company during their time in school, and by the time he reached age twenty-nine, Fuller had become a millionaire.

All was not well, however, with the Fuller family. Although

his relentless drive and sharp business acumen had enabled
him to become wealthy at a young age, his marriage, health,
and personal integrity all took a big hit. His discontent drove
him to reevaluate his life, and as a result, he renewed his marriage and committed his life to Jesus Christ.

He and his wife then made a momentous decision, the very
one I had been contemplating: they chose to sell everything
they owned, give the proceeds to the poor, and look for a new
life mission. His story warmed my sacrificial heart. I even wondered if I had found my mentor.

The Fullers eventually moved to Koinonia Farm, a Christian
community near Americus, Georgia, founded by Clarence
Jordan. There they began learning about how to apply Christ's
teaching in practical ways. During their time at Koinonia, the
Fullers helped begin several ministry initiatives, including
a housing enterprise that built affordable homes for lower-
income families.

Fuller and his family moved to Africa in 1973 to test the
housing model he'd helped develop, and in just a few years,
the project enjoyed such great success that he decided to expand it worldwide. The family returned to the United States
in 1976 and soon thereafter launched Habitat for Humanity.
Fuller built his ministry around what he called "the theology
of the hammer," described like this:

> This theology is about bringing a wide diversity of
> people, churches, and other organizations together
> to build houses and establish viable and dynamic
> communities. It is acknowledging that differences
> of opinion exist on numerous subjects—political,

philosophical, and theological—but that we can find common ground in using a hammer as an instrument to manifest God's love. As we focus on working together to build a house, we realize that the things that make us the same become more important than the things that keep us apart. Putting the theology of the hammer into practice will help us eliminate poverty housing while joining in fellowship and being of service to those in need.

As I finished reading the book, closed its covers and set it down, I knew I had to get in touch with Millard Fuller. I thought that if anyone could give me the guidance I so desperately needed, it had to be him. So I wrote him a letter. I told him that I wanted to send some money to him and that I wanted to find out where the greatest needs of the day might be. But also, I wanted to ask his advice about our own situation.

I didn't at all expect the answer I received.

Is There Just One Path?

In my letter, I asked Fuller whether he thought the path he had taken—selling everything he had and giving away all the proceeds to the poor—might be the right path for every believer of financial means. I asked him directly: Would he counsel all wealthy Christians to make the same decision he had made?

I sent off my letter and waited nervously for his reply. I felt tremendously excited when, not long afterward, I received his answer. This was it!

In his letter, Fuller admitted that, yes, God does lead some people to forsake everything they have for His kingdom. For him and his family, that decision brought a sense of purpose and a sort of relational glue that they could not have acquired in any other way.

So far, so good!

Fuller then cautioned me about the peril of riches. Because money gives its owners a measure of independence, it also can lead them to start depending upon it instead of upon God. While Fuller didn't use these exact words to say it, his caution reminded me of the very first temptation to godless independence that took place in the Garden of Eden. Satan enticed Adam and Eve to fall by promising them that they could become "like God" if they would just disobey God and eat the forbidden fruit. Money has some of that same power, the ability to give its owners the option of independent action—they can become "like God," choosing for themselves what they will do and how they will act, without reference to God.

> *If all Christians divested themselves of their money, then who would fund the work of God's kingdom?*

I really *loved* this letter! Its words deeply touched my heart. And so I got ready to read the message I fully expected and that my heart longed to see, something like, "Steve, thanks so much for writing. I sense you're in a very similar place to where I was years ago. So yes, I would counsel you to sell all you have and give it to the poor. And then find out where God would have you serve."

Except that's not what he said.

Who Will Fund the Work?

Millard Fuller did not counsel me to sell all we owned and give the money to the poor. He explained that he had come to see through his work with Habitat for Humanity that if *all* Christians gave up their wealth, it would cause a huge problem for the work of Christ worldwide. If all Christians divested themselves of their money, he asked, then who would fund the work of God's kingdom?

Well... I... had never really thought of it like that before.

Fuller's letter became a seminal experience for me, a two-by-four to the side of my head. I had felt *certain* that he would counsel me to sell our estate and give all the money to the poor. Isn't that what he and his family had done? Isn't that what Jesus had counseled the rich young ruler to do? Didn't that idea fill my imagination with longing?

But there it was, something very different from what I had expected, in black and white: "What I've come to see is that if all Christians in the world should rid themselves of their wealth, who would God have to fund His kingdom?"

Almost at that very moment, a brand-new idea entered my brain. *Hmm*, I thought, *maybe there is a purpose to all of this.*

God's Surprising Way

That letter from Millard Fuller had a profound impact on me. While it didn't answer all my questions or provide me with a detailed road map for my future, it clearly did stimulate some new thinking and call into question some old assumptions. I didn't at all receive the answer I had expected, but isn't that often God's way?

In fact, isn't it *usually* His way?

John T. Faris, an American author and clergyman born in 1871, once wrote, "The future is a closed book. Sometimes we wish that we might read that book and so know the events of years to come. But we seldom think how God is foreshadowing our future, that each event of every day has its own meaning and its own bearing upon our lives."[*]

I certainly wanted to read that book! I wanted to know the events of the years to come. I wanted to know—right then and there, in black and white—*What does God want us to do?* And Faris was right; I couldn't imagine at the time how God was foreshadowing the future for us. Faris continues:

> Why, then, don't we enter each day in the spirit of an explorer of unknown lands? We can look on everything that comes to us, whether duty or success or misfortune, as a treasure laden with vast

---

[*] John T. Faris in *How Great Thou Art: 365 Reasons Why God Is Awesome*, eds. Steven Halliday and William Travis (Sisters, OR: Multnomah Press, 1999), 349.

possibilities of blessing. We do not need to resign ourselves to thinking, *We do not know what this day may bring,* as though that truth holds out a forecast only of disappointment and defeat. We can open our eyes to see the ultimate good which God will bring to us through the events whose meaning is now so uncertain.

I especially like how Faris ended his thought: "We have every reason to live in hope and certainty. When our lives are yielded to God's leading, there will be good and only good. We must expect it. It will come."

Yes, it will. And sometimes, I discovered, it may come even through an unexpected sermon that I myself would preach.

11

THE SHREWD STEWARD

For sixteen years as a pastor, I avoided preaching on the parable of the shrewd steward. I just could never understand why Jesus would commend an unethical steward who changes the books so that people will favor him after his fraud costs him his job.

One Sunday in November of 1995, that was the assigned text in our church's lectionary. I was about to punt once again, as I always did whenever Luke 16:1–8 came around, but this time I kept looking at it over several days. And then, quite suddenly, I got an aha moment. I noticed in Jesus's words something I had never noticed before:

> The master commended the dishonest manager because he had acted shrewdly. For the people of this world are more shrewd in dealing with their own kind than are the people of the light. (verse 8)

The children of the world are more shrewd than are the children of the light.

It dawned on me that Jesus did not commend the character's unethical behavior, but rather praised his creativity and resourcefulness in dealing with his difficult situation. As Jesus looked around at the people of this world, He saw them employ a tremendous amount of effort, creativity, and resourcefulness—shrewdness—as they sought to achieve their goals.

But what did He see when He looked around at His own children, the children of the light? Did He see that same creativity and resourcefulness? Sadly, no. And so He grieved that the people of this world are far more innovative and imaginative in accomplishing their own goals and purposes than are His children in accomplishing His goals and purposes. "My own children lack that creative and resourceful spark," He lamented.

This new insight prompted an uncomfortable question for me. When it comes to the purposes of God, why do we as Christ's children seem to leave our brains at the front door of the church? Do we think it's carnal to draw from the knowledge and best practices of the world outside? Or do we fear that if we tap into the creativity within us as men and women made in His image, we'll somehow start glorying in our own gifts or drift away from "the faith that was once for all entrusted to the saints" (Jude 1:3)?

Are we too lazy? Or do we just fear new things? If that's the problem, then how do we react when we hear God himself say, "See, I am doing a new thing! Now it springs up; do you not perceive it? I am making a way in the desert and streams in the wasteland" (Isaiah 43:19)?

As I pondered both the Lord's lament and His commendation of the shrewd steward, I finally came to understand that the Lord did not praise the man for what he did, but for the imaginative way in which he pulled it off.

And that's when I finally swallowed hard and decided to preach on this previously off-limits text.

I spoke about how we are the most creative, resourceful people on the planet when we want something. Imagine a husband and wife at the dinner table. He tells her he would like a new car. She says that she needs a new washer and dryer. They both agree they can't afford both. That night, the husband tosses and turns, trying to figure a way to satisfy both of their desires. And then it hits him.

The next morning, he shares his creative idea with his wife. "Honey," he says, "I spent all night thinking about how I can get that new car and you can get your new washer and dryer. First, we sell our car and take $5,000 from its sale and put that money in the bank. Second, we lease a new car at Bud's Auto, with just $1,000 down—we'd be paying less than we are now. Then we take the rest of the money and put it in a high-interest savings account and we borrow on that account, rather than using a credit card to buy the washer and dryer. We'd get an effective interest rate of only 2 percent, rather than the 18 percent on the card, because it is secured by our deposit! It's like stealing money from the bank!" And so both the creative husband and his receptive wife get what they want.

But what happens when God wants us to use some of our resources for His purposes? It's like we're in elementary school. We don't bother to think, *Are there other, better ways of doing this?*

Jesus would say that we're just not shrewd enough—and He really wishes that we were.

An Innovative Partnership

Whenever the topic of stewardship comes up, nearly everyone always assumes money is the focus. But biblical stewardship involves a lot more than a person's finances. God wants us to creatively steward *everything* He gives us, most of which has little to do with money. He calls upon us to innovatively use our skills, gifts, abilities, hobbies, and networks, in addition to our wealth, to partner with Him in accomplishing His mission in the world.

Pastor Walt Kallestad from Community Church of Joy in Glendale, Arizona, once formed a motorcycle group for his church. Do you know why? He wanted to create an appealing back door to entice a group of people into the church who otherwise almost certainly never would choose to enter through the front door.

One member of our own church stewarded his business connections to benefit the kingdom. One day I got a call from my cousin-in-law, Carlos Saez, who needed some new mattresses for an orphanage he oversees in Ensenada, Mexico. "I have a member in my church who sells foam rubber products," I told him. "I'll see what I can do."

So I made a call. "Mike, do you have any contacts who could get us some mattresses for an orphanage in Ensenada?" I asked.

"Let me make a few calls," he replied. One of the vendors Mike contacted not only sold us mattresses at cost, but donated several more.

That's the kind of shrewdness I think Jesus wants us to employ. I didn't ask Mike to donate money; I asked him to tap his network to see what we might accomplish to bless some poor children in Ensenada.

Couldn't we do the same kind of thing with our hobbies and the resources we use in their pursuit? How do you think God could use a boat or a vacation home for the benefit of needy people or pastors and the expansion of His kingdom?

> *It's not the size of what we have that matters; it's when we surrender whatever we have to God that He makes the miracle happen.*

How can you, as a man or woman of the light, act shrewdly for Jesus? How can you stir your gray matter to get resourceful and creative in using your God-given wealth, talent, connections, and even hobbies for the work of God's kingdom?

It doesn't really matter how much you have or how large your reservoir of resources may be. Remember the story of the little boy with the five loaves and two fish (Mark 14:15–20)? Jesus took what the boy had and multiplied it into something far greater. It's not the size of what we have that matters; it's when we surrender whatever we have to God that He makes the miracle happen.

Maybe this is a new thought for you. Maybe you've never considered how Jesus may want you to act more shrewdly with your resources. If that's the case, embrace the idea rather than lamenting what might have been. Our whole life is a process of becoming more of what God created us to be. As C. S. Lewis said, being a Christian is not about being perfect, it's about getting better each day. It's identifying the things we've claimed for ourselves that we need to transfer to God for His possible use. We've held on tight for fear that we might lose it, but by being able to live with it freely, by releasing it to God, we'll see what He wants to do with it.

What kind of miracle do you think God might want to do through your own five loaves and two fish?

Full Integration

My long-delayed insight into the story of the shrewd steward, along with the letter from Millard Fuller, finally enabled me to see how I could begin to fully integrate my faith and my wealth. Until then, I did not live with the two in a cohesive way. They remained bifurcated, with my faith over here and my wealth over there. While my faith always informed some aspects of how I used our wealth, I had never lived with the two in a fully unified manner. I typically approached my wealth and my faith as two separate things.

Wholeness came into my life when I realized that there could be (and should be) a seamlessness between the two. So I guess you could say that I owe this healthy integration to a creative tag-team effort between Millard Fuller and the shrewd steward. I must say, I find it a whole lot more satisfying than the former schizophrenic division!

And I suspect you will, too.

12

THE MILLION-DOLLAR CHECK

I've always had the unique ability to lose whatever pen I carry in my pocket. Motivated by that reality, one day I went out and bought a Montblanc, thinking that buying a pen that cost $100 would greatly reduce my chances of losing it.

And my plan worked... for about six months. And then I lost the thing.

I told my wife about my missing pen, hoping that she would keep an eye out for it. After all, this was no Bic. It was a Montblanc. It had to turn up.

For a few days, I searched high and low for that missing writing implement. I looked in every nook and cranny where I might have gone the previous week. After I ran out of places to search and could think of no other action to take, I went to the store and bought another pen (remembering that buying an expensive one had not cured my proclivity for losing them).

Six months later, I found the lost pen. It had fallen into the blackness of the bottom of my attaché case and had hidden there all the time. Can you guess how I reacted? I jumped for joy, knowing I had *not* lost forever my beautiful, black, missing-in-action Montblanc.

When I proudly presented my discovery to Susie, we

celebrated together its unexpected return. Although its re-appearance seemed a little to me like the homecoming of a black sheep, I realized that in this case, the sheep hadn't wandered away; rather, its oblivious shepherd had simply let it fall for a short while into a dark pit.

But in any case, *it was back!* And so we rejoiced.

At that moment, I had some of the same feelings that must have washed over the woman described in Luke 15 when she recovered a lost silver coin. When she first realized it had gone missing, she lit a lamp, swept her house, and searched carefully until she found it. When at last it turned up, she excitedly called her friends and neighbors together and said, "Rejoice with me; I have found my lost coin" (verse 9).

Who doesn't know the feeling of great joy at discovering (or rediscovering) some prized item? At those times, just like the woman, we want to shout to our neighbors and friends, "Rejoice with me! I have found my [fill in the blank]!" It's a great feeling.

But what can you do when you have severe doubts that you can share your joyous news with anyone, fearful of their reaction? Unfortunately, I know that feeling, too.

From Jubilant Celebration to Cheery Whimper

One summer several years ago, my wife's family decided to sell a group of office buildings, the first time the family had made such a decision in our (then) twenty-three years of marriage. After the sale closed, we received a check for a million dollars.

Distributions from the family business normally got spread out throughout the year, so never before had we received such a large check.

The two of us reacted just like the widow who found her coin, or like a man who just heard on the radio he'd won the lottery. I took Susie outside the house, sat her on a bench, and had her hold up the check so I could take a picture of it. We felt like having a party!

Sadly, however, that's where our little celebration ended—on the bench, outside our home. Unlike the woman who excitedly told her friends about her good fortune, we knew of *no one* with whom we could share our joy. We feared that anyone we might call would take the news as gloating or bragging. And so instead of enjoying a jubilant celebration among friends, we shared a jolly whimper on an outdoor bench. We had no one to help us complete our joy.

In his book *Reflections on the Psalms*, C. S. Lewis memorably discusses the connection between joy and the necessity of celebration:

> I think we delight to praise what we enjoy because *the praise not merely expresses but completes the enjoyment; it is its appointed consummation.* It is not out of compliment that lovers keep on telling one another how beautiful they are; the delight is incomplete till it is expressed. It is frustrating to have discovered a new author and not to be able to tell anyone how good he is; to come suddenly, at the turn of the road, upon some mountain valley of unexpected grandeur

and then to have to keep silent because the people with you care for it no more than for a tin can in the ditch; to hear a good joke and find no one to share it with.

Delight calls for communal expression, just like a funny joke calls for a receptive audience. Good news clamors to be shared. Just because the news concerns a wonderfully un-expected financial boon does not disqualify the event from some kind of corporate celebration. If it did, then it seems very strange indeed that Jesus would approvingly compare the joy of a woman finding a sum of money (which is what a coin *is*) to the joy felt in heaven whenever a man or woman finds new life in Jesus.

With whom do you feel safe enough to celebrate your blessings, in a way that allows all of you together to give boisterous thanks to God and thus complete the joy He wants you to experience?

I suppose the real question here is, why did Susie and I fear to share our good news with friends? Why didn't we think we could call up fellow believers from church and tell them of our million-dollar check? I think the answer to that question has to do with safety. We doubted that we could tell our good news to our Christian friends without getting censured in one fashion or another. And so we kept quiet.

An Added Burden (Cue the Violins)

In at least one way, wealth creates an added burden before God for Christians of capacity. Yes, I know—everyone should have such hardships. I recall the conversation in *Fiddler on the Roof* between a young Perchik and the mature Tevye. The revolutionary Perchik declares, "Money is the world's curse." The father Tevye replies, "May the Lord smite me with it. And may I never recover."

I get it.

But the burden is still real.

Although believers with significant financial resources want to be treated just like everyone else, they often get elevated to a status they would reject if possible. They don't want to be seen as different or especially favored; many are average people who, in one way or another, simply wound up with a lot of money. While they long for a normal life with normal friends, they tend to get placed into a category that distances them from both.

This fact helps to explain why we didn't reach out to others with our good news. While we wanted others to share our excitement over this new milestone, we doubted that telling anyone about a million-dollar check would generate the kind of excitement we desired. Experience already had taught us we probably would get instead something more along these lines:

- "Oh... uh, well, um... don't spend it all in one place. Heh, heh, heh. Umm, unless you want to give it to *me!*"
- "You know, this could be providential. I just heard this morning about a worthy ministry in Borneo that needs a million dollars right away!"
- "I see. Well, just remember, Steve, that the love of money is the root of all kinds of evil. Don't get too excited about it."
- "I'm happy for you. Really. 'Bye."

The Bible instructs us to "rejoice with those who rejoice" (Romans 12:15), and when the Lord gives someone an extra measure of resources to use for His kingdom, all who belong to Him should truly be able to rejoice with them, for "The blessing of the LORD brings wealth, and He adds no trouble to it" (Proverbs 10:22). The Lord's blessing in this area is just as deserving of collective rejoicing and celebration as any of His other blessings.

So let me ask: With whom do you feel safe enough to celebrate your blessings, in a way that allows all of you *together* to give boisterous thanks to God and thus complete the joy He wants you to experience? If you don't have such friends, you need to find some. None of us is an island; we all need encouragement to follow whatever track God has us on.

Remember, too, that there is an even deeper joy in wisely using some of your resources for kingdom purposes. Don't forget that Jesus used the story of the woman's great joy in finding her lost coin to tell the surrounding crowd, "I tell you, there is rejoicing in the presence of the angels of God over one sinner who repents" (Luke 15:10). Tax collectors and sinners were in that crowd. So were Pharisees, men who "dearly loved their money," according to Luke (16:14, NLT). And Jesus used a story about money to point them all to one of the deepest joys of all, found when sinners come to repentance.

I don't know when you might be getting a million-dollar check. But if or when the moment comes, don't neglect to celebrate the blessings God gives you—*all* of them—even if it takes a little creativity to do so.

13

SAFE COMMUNITIES

C hristians of capacity do not have many safe places where they can safely go without fear of being judged, getting caught up in the game of one-upmanship, or finding themselves accosted by someone who wants to get something from them.

You would hope the church could be such a place.

Too often, it's not.

Churches often ignore, use, or abuse their wealthy members. Pastors often come from very humble means, and the idea of believers with wealth tends to intimidate them. Whether this intimidation stems from a perverted theological view of wealth or an issue of perceived differences in class, many pastors tend to either ignore or badger the wealthy. Their preaching can almost become abusive as they subliminally convey that money is the root of all evil and the spawn of Satan himself. Whenever a big capital campaign arrives, however, suddenly calls go out for the "filthy lucre" that at other times of the year is said to corrupt one's soul.

> *Christians of capacity must find safe places*
> *where they can learn how to joyfully steward*
> *all that God has given them.*

The difficulty that Susie and I encountered most acutely in the church is that those who shared our values didn't share our means, and so they didn't fully understand our questions of how one might become a faithful steward of these God-entrusted resources. Meanwhile, those outside the church who shared our means didn't share our values, and therefore couldn't comprehend why this was such a struggle for us.

When Susie and I found the Gathering, we found a fellowship of Christian philanthropists of similar means and like values who totally understood our questions and concerns. When I described the Gathering to members of my small group after our first experience with it in 1996, the men asked me to define this apparently glorious and life-giving organization. I could only say, "It's like an AA group of people of means, each one struggling in their own way as to what it means to be blessed with more than they need." I'll never forget the dumbfounded look on their confused faces. Here we had the brass ring, their life dream, to have more money than one could need—and we felt *troubled* by it?

Neither the world nor most members in our churches will ever fully understand the angst and concerns that Christians of capacity feel regarding their wealth. We know that wealth can become purposeless, ultimately turning into a curse that can destroy marriages and ruin children. Those of us called to steward wealth fear that these terrifying stories could become our own.

That is why we need to be involved with safe communities such as the Gathering, Generous Giving, and the National Christian Foundation. Christians of capacity must find safe places where they can learn how to joyfully steward all that God has given them. We need others who can help us find a cohesive vision with the power to energize our whole family.

Finding a Safe Place

A good shepherd purposefully finds safe places for his sheep, where they can relax and find refreshment. The Gathering has been such a place for Susie and me.

This year, we celebrate our nineteenth year since we started coming to the Gathering. We are far different and more confident people today than when we first came!

Prior to our introduction to the Gathering, Susie and I lived very confused lives. We never felt comfortable in our own skin as Christians of capacity. On the one hand, we felt thankful for the many blessings that God had given us. On the other, we "hid our light under the basket," as we also lived with guilt and embarrassment over those many blessings.

For more than a decade, we longed for a community where we could find commonality of values and means, where our questions and concerns regarding wealth and the Christian's responsibility would be fully understood and openly encouraged. During that decade, we struggled to find a harmonious balance between the tensions of joy and responsibility, blessing and privilege, grace and duty—the very tensions that wealth and faith created within us.

When Susie and I learned in 1996 that such a community existed, we began to weep. We had longed and prayed for a shepherd, or shepherds, who could walk alongside us to help show us how we could learn to live wisely, purposely, and joyfully with the many blessings God had given us. The issues of wealth for Susie and me were as much psychological as they were spiritual and practical.

Susie did not grow up in a family that understood biblical stewardship. Though her parents were kindhearted, generous people, they were at best communitarians who felt they had a responsibility to give back to the community that had helped them to succeed. I, on the other hand, had embraced a piety that saw poverty as next to godliness, with the rich young ruler as the only available paradigm for wealthy believers. To say we struggled long and hard with our distorted views of wealth and its purposes is an understatement!

By the time we heard about the Gathering, we already had been married for twenty years. To some degree, we were just beginning to emerge from a wilderness of confusion. But becoming, at last, part of the Gathering's community greatly and wonderfully accelerated our journey into wholeness and life.

Through our fellowship with other Christians of capacity, we soon realized that we weren't alone in our quest to harmoniously integrate our faith and our wealth. At that time, the dot-com bubble was making rich men of a lot of Christians. As their businesses got sold, they began receiving huge cash distributions and bonuses. Some said they felt like a deer caught in the headlights. They wondered, "Whoa, what do we do?" For the first time in our lives, we could safely emerge from our self-imposed isolation and be totally honest about who we were, without fear of appearing to brag or belittle others.

Susie and I also learned we could give up the burden of being the sole source for one another's inspiration and teaching. The Gathering has helped to shepherd us both so that we can at last begin to grow together and develop a shared vision for what God wants us to be and to do.

The Gathering also provided at least one other service for us, as do similar communities of faith. As a husband and a father (and yes, as a pastor), I realized that I am not very good at inspiring my family to live out a vision as God's steward. Most spouses and parents, I believe, would say the same. Inspiring one's spouse or children is something like a prophet who returns home but finds a cool reception among his own countrymen. If we are to remain truly inspired, we have to find people we can truly trust to speak into our lives. It may sound strange, but most of us are able to receive truth and encouragement from those outside the family circle far more readily than we are from those within that circle.

The year we discovered the Gathering, we felt a healing within our soul. We finally met people who shared our values, had similar means, were asking the same questions we were, and who struggled in many of the same areas.

Pounding in the Nails

A powerful speaker at the Gathering once likened our spiritual journey to what happens each year at his summer cottage on the East Coast. Every spring, he makes a special trip to the cottage in order to pound in nails that have come loose during the rough winter. Those nails hold shingles in place on the side of the house, shingles that have become warped and unfastened.

In a sense, that is what the church is for. As we live exposed to the unfriendly environment of our society, vis-à-vis TV, radio, or toxic acquaintances, our vision and our values can become warped. The nails of our faith work loose a little, and we need to pound them back in. How do we accomplish that? By renewing our vision as to why we are here and whom we are called to serve. The fuel for all purposeful living is vision. Without a vision, the people perish. Vision is what captivates, inspires, and challenges to us to live as faithful stewards of God.

But vision is a renewable resource. It needs to be continually fed, lifted up, inspired, and awakened. Safe communities provide this for us by keeping alive and renewing the vision of who we are in Christ and what God has called us to be and do with the wealth He has entrusted to us.

With each passing year, we come away refreshed in our purposes for what God may have before us. It is also our hope and belief that groups like the Gathering will serve in a similar way for our children and their spouses, so that we may continue to grow as a family in the shared values and purposes that God has given to us.

Though our journey is far from over, we've already traveled a long way. The confusion and discomfort that once drove us to the Gathering's doors have long since ceased to be our primary motivation. We now come to green pastures looking to relax and enjoy the greater blessings of special friendships and the opportunity to be reminded once again of the truths—whose we are and why we're blessed—that so define us.

14

THE FIVE PURPOSES OF WEALTH

F or just a moment, imagine that you're at a Celine Dion concert. As she walks on stage, she greets the audience with an unexpected apology.

"Ladies and gentlemen," she says, "before I perform for you tonight, I want to offer my sincerest apologies for having been gifted with this rare and exceptional voice. It is not my purpose to demean any of you who cannot sing as well as I can. I merely want to share with you a gift that God has given to me."

Ludicrous, isn't it? It would never happen. Yet that is how many Christians of capacity feel. They get very apologetic for what they have, so much so that they hide their possessions so others won't discover their wealth—and possibly condemn them for their supposed excesses.

For me, the first step to finding joy was to begin the process of integrating my wealth and my faith. The opposite of love of wealth is total indifference to wealth, as though it has no meaning for us. But Jesus says our wealth *does* have meaning, just like any other divine gift. He wants us to use it to bless others, to honor God, to build His kingdom, to provide for our families and, yes, to enjoy. I had to realize that my wealth had purpose, *just as much purpose as my being a pastor.*

The Seminal Moment

When I resigned my call to the church in 1996, Susie expressed an interest in moving to what was known as the richie neighborhood. She'd wanted to do so eight years before, but I had said, "No way!" But by this time I had reached a point where I could agree without feeling ashamed to do so.

We moved into the new neighborhood immediately after we left the church. We exchanged a nice, middle-class executive home for a house in an upper-class neighborhood made up of 75 percent custom homes.

By this point, I had started to feel very good about our faith/ wealth integration. I had just helped launched the predecessor to the National Christian Foundation's Southern California office, and at the same time, the spigots of the family business started to really let go. We began to deal with real money— more money than what we knew what to do with. Our capacity quickly exceeded our vision.

I spent most of my time attending any seminar or lecture that remotely related to stewardship. It all felt both fun and exciting. My entrepreneurial spirit got really ramped up, which I loved. I began to see how broad the Christian world really is. When you pastor a church, your world is confined primarily to four corners. You have little exposure to what Christ is doing in the larger body. Now I started to see all sorts of very dynamic Christian laypeople doing exciting things. My world started growing.

You've heard of six degrees of separation? In Orange County, it's two degrees. I began making a number of new friends. While

THE FIVE PURPOSES OF WEALTH

I didn't go around wearing the Segerstrom badge—I still say, "Being Steve Perry and $2.50 gets me a cup of coffee"—Susie's family name did garner some instant credibility for me.

Once the money really started coming in, I realized that giving 15 percent, our custom until then, didn't seem like enough. We still gave out of our abundance. "Going forward," I said to Susie, "I think we need to extend our giving." We talked about hosting some Christian artists at the performing arts center as a way of tithing our influence, using her family name for God's kingdom. We also discussed doing pastor and spouse retreats.

"Why don't we commit to giving 25 percent of our income?" I asked.

"Okay," she said without batting an eye.

When I helped start the NCF office in California, I didn't realize I was on the front wave of a whole new movement. I'm usually not on the front wave of anything. I'm one of those guys who tend to get onto the wave only after the Holy Spirit has already passed through. When I resigned my call from the church, I left with the idea of helping to get the NCF office launched and using it as a means to engage other Christians of capacity who struggled with the same issues of wealth that Susie and I had experienced. The idea was to create a safe place to talk.

Unfortunately, it didn't produce as much fruit as I'd hoped, at least, not directly. We hosted lunches and brought in speakers. We wanted to bring Christians together to talk to one another and hear about novel and effective ways to "do stewardship." In hindsight, maybe that was a way of indirectly fulfilling my call from God. When God called me in 1971, He said to me, "Gather my people." I guess that's what I was trying to do, because I truly believe the Spirit of God moves mightily in and through community. And as I spoke to Christians from many backgrounds and perspectives, I began to learn much more about the purpose of wealth.

The Purpose of Wealth

Wealth has a clear divine purpose. My friend Ray Lyne, the founder and president of Lifestyle Giving, says that God designed wealth to bring blessing to God by honoring Him and to bless our neighbors by helping them. The Scriptures make it clear that God has at least five purposes for the wealth He provides.

1. *To glorify God* (Proverbs 3:9; 2 Corinthians 9:11, 12)

   How do you use your wealth to glorify God? One of the best ways is to put it to work in ways that prompt others to thank God for your generosity and to manage it in a God-honoring way.

2. *To provide for your family* (1 Timothy 5:8; Proverbs 27:23–27; Titus 3:14)

   Many people might not know or acknowledge their daily financial responsibility to care for their families, but Christians have no such excuse.

3. *To support His church* (1 Timothy 5:17, 18; Galatians 6:10)

We must never forget that the church, a community of believers in Jesus, has always been God's frontline tool for reaching the world with the Gospel. It is also the primary means by which God nurtures us and our families, as well as His main vehicle for reaching out and serving our communities.

4. *To bless my neighbor* (Galatians 6:10; 1 John 3:17–18; Luke 10:25–37)

"Wealth unused might as well not exist," said Aesop, echoing the Bible's insistence that those blessed with wealth are to use it to help the less fortunate. People with a genuine heart for God tend to develop God's habits of giving.

5. *To enjoy the blessings of God* (Genesis 2:8–9; Ecclesiastes 2:24–25, 5:18–20; 1 Timothy 6:17)

Satisfaction in work and enjoyment in life are both gifts from the hand of God. Like all of His good gifts, we enjoy them most when we express to Him our deepest thanks.

I don't know if it's kosher for a Lutheran to quote the Westminster Shorter Catechism, but I think it comes very close to the truth when it states that "the chief end of man is to glorify God [the first of the purposes of wealth] and to enjoy Him forever [the final purpose of wealth]." Living between those two poles has a natural way of helping us to hit the target.

Why are you *wealthy?*

When you consider carefully the five purposes of wealth, you see it's not all service. In fact, we serve God best when our wealth lives in harmony with God's purposes. The goal therefore is to redeem our wealth in positive ways so that it becomes viewed as a gift to be used for God's glory, purposes, and pleasure.

And that makes me wonder: Could this be our primary act of worship?

Why Are You Wealthy?

You may not think of yourself as wealthy, but let me assure you that each of us *is* rich, both in God's eyes and in the eyes of the world.

I once asked someone, "How do you define wealthy?"

He responded, "Someone whose income is in the top 1 percent."

Would you agree with him?

"Did you know that if you make $27,000 a year," I asked, "you would be in the top 1 percent of income producers throughout the course of human history? And that you are in the top 3 percent of all people who live today?"

There's no question that we're all wealthy. The only real question to ask is *why*. Why are we wealthy?

Why are *you* wealthy?

I believe that God is investing in each of us, whether ten talents, five talents, or just one (see Matthew 25:14–30). Whatever the size of your wealth, God is investing in you so that you may bear fruit for His glory and His kingdom throughout your lifetime.

15

GOD OWNS IT ALL
(AND HE MAKES SOME WEALTHY)

D uring Jesus's time, and even to our own day and age, there have been basically three worldviews on the issue of ownership of one's wealth. My friend Gary Moore of the Financial Seminary summarizes the three like this.

1.   *Plato's view: Society owns our wealth.*

   The revered Greek philosopher held the position that when we died, the state owned our wealth and therefore it should be used to serve the public good instead of getting handed down to our heirs or to whomever or wherever we wanted it to go. He taught that society would accomplish its purposes and goals through the accumulated wealth of individuals.

   Certainly, we hear this message loud and clear from our federal government in the form of estate tax laws. For all intents and purposes, we have called this liberal philosophy "socialism."

2.   *Rome's view: We are sole the owners of our wealth.*

   Rome insisted that as the sole owners of our wealth, we are free to do with our resources whatever we want to do with them:

save, spend wisely or foolishly, give them away. The choice is always ours to make. Rome believed that wealth had but one exclusive purpose—to serve our own goals and purposes.

In time, we have come to call this conservative philosophy "capitalism." Contrary to popular opinion, capitalism does have its compassionate side, called philanthropy. But philanthropy, for the most part, still abides by the Roman paradigm, since as a philanthropist, my wealth is mine to distribute as I choose.

3.   *The Judeo-Christian worldview: We manage God's wealth.*

Both Jews and Jesus taught what a friend of mine calls "stewardism." In stewardism, we never own the wealth we control; God does. We are merely stewards, trustees or managers of that wealth. Our goal in life, then, must be to use that wealth to accomplish whatever satisfies God's goals and purposes.

As a Christian, a follower of Christ, I naturally endorse the third view. And it starts with the truth that God owns everything.

God Owns It All

The Bible makes it clear that God owns everything He created, and since He created everything that exists, He owns everything in existence. Once in a while you may hear some nonsense about God "losing" ownership of the earth when Adam fell— the story goes that God deeded the earth to Adam and Adam lost the title deed of the planet to Satan when he disobeyed God in the Garden—but such an idea is totally foreign to Scripture.

> *Our goal in life must be to use the wealth*
> *we have been given to accomplish whatever*
> *satisfies God's goals and purposes.*

I don't want to bore you with a long list of Scripture texts, but just to be clear that God does in fact own it all, consider a few of them that teach exactly that.

"Who has given me anything that I need to pay back? Everything under heaven is mine," declares the Lord in emphatic terms (Job 41:11, NLT). The Hebrew term translated as "everything" means, well, "everything."

God reiterates His claim through the prophet Isaiah when He says, "My hands have made both heaven and earth; they and everything in them are mine. I, the LORD, have spoken!" (Isaiah 66:2, NLT).

The apostle Paul reminded his readers of this teaching with a quote from the Old Testament: "The earth is the Lord's, and everything in it" (1 Corinthians 10:26).

To make sure no one could make a mistake here, God gets even more detailed when He claims, "every animal of the forest is mine, and the cattle on a thousand hills. I know every bird in the mountains, and the creatures of the field are mine." How could you get much clearer? But He even gets more emphatic: "If I were hungry I would not tell you, for the world is mine, and all that is in it" (Psalm 50:9–12). God, of course, never gets hungry, but if He ever did, we'd never hear about it, because

He'd just dip into the vast resources that He made and continues to own.

So let's just agree to believe Him when He says, very simply, "All the earth is mine" (Exodus 19:5, ESV).

God Gives Some Wealth

God not only owns everything, He also has the right to give any portion of His wealth to anyone He chooses, for however long He chooses, for whatever reason He chooses. As an old Lutheran preacher, I don't necessarily like quoting a bunch of Bible verses in a row, but I do want to make the point, so here goes.

Proverbs declares, "The blessing of the LORD brings wealth, and He adds no trouble to it" (Proverbs 10.22). What brings wealth? God's blessing. A few chapters later we read, "Humility and the fear of the LORD bring wealth and honor and life" (Proverbs 22:4).

The writer of Ecclesiastes tells us that God gives some men "wealth and possessions," enabling them "to enjoy" what they own and to accept their lot in life and "be happy" in their work—and all of this he calls "a gift of God" (Ecclesiastes 5:19). Do all men receive this gift? No.

Hannah, the mother of the prophet Samuel, says in a great song of praise, "The LORD sends poverty and wealth" (1 Samuel 2:7). Centuries later, Hannah's prayer became a model for Mary, the mother of Jesus, in a beautiful prayer we call the Magnificat.

David, the famous forebear of Jesus, once said to the Lord,

"Wealth and honor come from you; you are the ruler of all things" (1 Chronicles 29:12).

And just so the people of Israel would never forget that God owns everything and gives wealth to whomever He chooses, Deuteronomy 8:17–18 reminds them, "You may say to yourself, 'My power and the strength of my hands have produced this wealth for me.' But remember the LORD your God, for it is He who gives you the ability to produce wealth."

A Dash through Biblical History

And how does this general principle about wealth play out in biblical history? We see it in action almost from the very beginning. The Bible introduces us to quite a few rich men who, Scripture declares, received their wealth from God himself:

- Job (Job 1:10)
- Abraham (Genesis 13:2)
- Isaac (Genesis 26:12–13)
- Israelites fleeing Egypt (Exodus 3:21–22)
- The Reubenites, the Gadites, and the half tribe of Manasseh (Joshua 22:6–8)
- Boaz (Ruth 2:1, NASB)
- David (1 Chronicles 29:28)
- Solomon (2 Chronicles 1:12)
- Hezekiah (2 Chronicles 32:29)
- Future children of God (Isaiah 60:5)
- Joseph of Arimathea (Matthew 27:57)

God owns it all, and He continues to give some rich portions of it to men and women of His choice.

Praise Him Either Way

Biblical scholars suggest that Jesus may not have come from a poor family, as many of us have always assumed. They point to the fact that Jesus was called "Rabbi," and men of that day didn't use the term loosely. Students had to pay to go to school to become a rabbi, or pay for a tutor to receive the required training. Scholars therefore conclude that Jesus may have come from a family of some means.

I don't know whether they're right, but either way, it points up the fact that God distributes His gifts of wealth as He chooses, for His own reasons. One might think that the King of the Universe would arrive with some means! What babies, after all, get presents of frankincense, gold, and myrrh? And what happened to those gifts after His birth?

But what if Jesus really didn't come from a family of means? It would only demonstrate, once again, that God owns it all—and to *some* He gives wealth. Our response is to praise Him either way:

> For all things come from You, and from Your hand we have given You. (1 Chronicles 29:14, NASB)

16

ALL IS SACRED TO GOD

M any years ago, I did something that prompted a former church member to question my pastoral purity. He confronted me and I freely admitted that I had done the very thing that so incensed him. And what was my infraction?

I'd bought a new car, a Chevy Citation. The man insisted that properly pious pastors should buy only used vehicles.

In a similar vein, many of us remember a time when it was considered ungodly for Christians to play cards, go to a movie, or drink anything containing alcohol. And true Christians never *danced*! Dancing was nothing more than "the vertical expression of a horizontal desire." A few jovial critics of this philosophy gently replied that, heavens no, Christians should never drink, lest dancing break out.

Not so long ago, many in the church considered all of these things "too worldly." They considered them nothing but evil entanglements in a fallen world destined for fiery destruction. How did they come to such a conviction? I believe that a big part of the problem was that they had come to believe something bequeathed to them by the Gnostics, false teachers who began troubling the early church shortly after its birth.

A Deadly Gift That Keeps on Giving

Gnostics thought of the material world as evil and acknowledged only spirit and knowledge as good. They taught that because human beings were imprisoned in physical bodies, only that unfortunate fact required them to interact with (evil) physical things. They saw food and shelter as necessary evils, never to be fully embraced or enjoyed.

The Gnostic path to "salvation" then logically involved a purging of all worldly influences in the hopes of ultimately arriving at a place of pure spirit. These ideas led them to divide the world between the secular and the sacred.

There is no secular area where God has no interest or concern. All that God has created, and still creates in and through each of us, is sacred to Him.

Strangely enough, such an unbiblical perspective has infected elements of the church throughout history, even to the present day. Today, it often reveals itself in the idea that anything not directly connected to church activity—work, home, car, vacation, you fill in the blank—is secular rather than sacred, which usually indicates a compromised life.

Have you ever met a Christian who believed that to fully serve God, you had to be in full-time Christian ministry? I have.

An outstanding ministry that I enthusiastically endorse insisted for a long time that if a believer really wanted to enjoy a life of significance, then he or she had to find a job in the church or in a parachurch group. It made a huge distinction between the sacred and the secular.

The ancient heresy of Gnosticism has very long tentacles.

Fortunately, Martin Luther awakened the church almost five hundred years ago to the proposition that every baptized believer is first a minister for God, whose pulpit just happens to be his or her place of work. He wrote, "The menial housework of a manservant or maidservant is often more acceptable to God than all the fastings and other works of a monk or priest, because the monk or priest lacks faith" (Luther, "On the Babylonian Captivity," 1520).

God does not long for more Christians to work vocationally in the church. These believers do not need a new job, but a new vision for where God already has placed them. Let me illustrate the point.

A local town reporter arrived at a new church construction site. The reporter approached one worker to ask what he was doing. "I'm laying brick," came the unenthusiastic reply. So the reporter went to a second man and asked the same question. Visibly annoyed, the worker responded, "Can't you see I'm building a wall?" Struggling to find a noteworthy story, the reporter tried once more. This time the worker laid down his brick and, with an expression of great delight on his face, replied, "I am building a cathedral for my God."

There is no secular area where God has no interest or concern. *All* that God has created, and still creates in and through each of us, is sacred to Him. God did not create an entire world so that we might embrace just a part of it and hold the majority of it at arm's length. For God, the whole world is sacred. It all belongs to Him. And He has a great desire to redeem all that is in His world—our vocation, our love life, our avocations, our talents, and yes, our wealth—so that they might live under His Lordship and serve His glory and honor His name.

Why Do We Have Bodies?

Have you ever wondered why God created us with bodies? He could have created us as spirits without bodies, but He didn't. Why not?

Apparently, He doesn't care much for the secular/sacred divide. And in part, at least, that's why He created a material world. While Gnosticism prioritizes the spiritual over the material, we live in a material world that God declared to be "good" the moment He created it. We are *material* beings with *material* needs. And God calls us to use our *material* blessings to honor Him, help our neighbor, care for His creation, and even use some of it for our material enjoyment. Consequently, shunning material things as though they were ungodly not only denies what and who we are, but also opposes God's very purposes for our very *material* existence.

God never calls wealth a sin. Not in the Old Testament, not in the New Testament. Nowhere.

What He calls sin is the *misuse* of material wealth.

In fact, God identifies Himself as the giver of all material wealth (Deuteronomy 8:18; 1 Chronicles 29:12). But just like every other gift from God, wealth comes with a calling to honor God. And the gift is not universal.

Certainly, God calls us to a life of selflessness. But does selflessness mean a total sublimation of self-interest, or is it more a matter of becoming obedient to God's will whenever His will conflicts with our personal desires and pursuits? Did Jesus sin in the Garden of Gethsemane when He asked His Father—not once, but three times—to "take this cup from me"? No, He didn't. But as a physical human being living in a material world, the horror of the onrushing cross caused Him to cry out for deliverance... if God would so will it. But God did not so will it, and so Jesus freely submitted Himself to the will of His Father. He really meant it when earlier He had said, "I have come down from heaven not to do my will but to do the will of Him who sent me" (John 6:38, NIV). If Jesus had not willingly submitted His body to the purposes of His Father, you wouldn't be reading this book.

The Beauty of All Creation

We can all agree that we see God in a beautiful sunrise or a majestic sunset, but can we not also see Him in the beauty of things created through the exercise of our God-given talents and abilities—including those things that exist outside of the church?

My mind drifts back to the craftsmen of Moses's day whom God gifted with skill and ability to build the wilderness tabernacle. Was their work any less holy when they applied the same craft and skill to creating goods for the daily use of God's people? Too often, however, we decide that God has little appreciation for those who use their gifts and talents outside of the work of the church or parachurch. I know this because we call their work "secular," often a code word for "less godly."

The same mistaken spirit gets carried over to how we view the world around us. We can celebrate God's beauty in great artwork displayed in museums or in cathedrals, but often have less appreciation for the God-given skill it takes to create a finely sculpted car or the craftsmanship that goes into a beautiful home. But why should the former be any more "holy" than the latter? The difference between that which is holy and that which is not has nothing to do with the nature of the object, but simply with the person for whom the object exists.

In the third installment of the Indiana Jones films, Indy and a horde of others pursue the Holy Grail, the cup of Christ from the Last Supper. Toward the end of the movie, he and his Nazi sympathizer competitors come upon a vast display of jewel-studded chalices, cups made of precious metals, and one very ordinary-looking clay cup.

The villains of the movie (and yes, many in the church) automatically assume that the cup that outwardly appears to be most precious has to be the cup of Christ, but those who drink from the jewel-studded chalices do not live long. They "chose poorly," according to the knight who guards the cups. Only the ordinary clay cup, the cup of a carpenter, was the true and Holy Grail. What made the cup "holy" was not its material being, but its status as something set apart for God's work.

All work and *all* things can be holy before God, and therefore beautiful, so long as they have been received from God for the work of God. God is a giver of beauty, and beauty always conveys hope and promise. If the whole world belongs to God, then beauty in *all* its forms and expression is a wonderful gift from God.

Called to a Sacred Work

The whole world is sacred to God. He made it. He owns it. He wants all of it to live under His reign and His lordship. Our job is to help make that happen with whatever resources He has entrusted to us.

Our job becomes difficult, however, when we believe that some things He made are unworthy of His kingdom or of existing under His lordship. *What does my wealth have to do with the Kingdom of God?* we may wonder.

Christ came to redeem the world. He didn't come to redeem souls only. That's why the Lord mentions in both testaments His unwavering commitment to preparing a "new heavens and a new earth" (Isaiah 65:17; 2 Peter 3:13). Why would He ask us to spend our time and money to partner with Him in building His kingdom if someday it was all going to burn, anyway? While I believe that what we build for Christ is going to be tested with fire (see 1 Corinthians 3), I also believe that what remains will somehow beautify and enrich the new earth.

This follows the pattern described in 1 Corinthians 15:35–53, where God declares His plan to take these old, "corruptible" bodies of ours and turn them into new, "incorruptible" ones. If anything, those new bodies will be more "material" and substantial what we have now—the difference between "unclothed" now and "clothed" then (2 Corinthians 5:4).

I have no idea exactly how this works. Frankly, it's beyond my comprehension. But I do know that God wastes nothing. He takes our junk and turns it into treasure. God is the world's greatest recycler! And He invites us to take our resources, as material as they may be, and gladly join Him in His work of reclamation.

It's a sacred work.

17

A FAITH JOURNEY

E veryone has a different path.
    I have come to see that how we live with our wealth, regardless of its size, is as much a faith journey as our walk with Christ. Just as not all of us are gifted to be pastors, teachers, evangelists, or administrators, so God has different paths for how each of us should live with the wealth He gives us.

Those who describe the Christ walk in terms of a single one-size-fits-all formula greatly oversimplify the truth. God has different paths for each of us and it is our responsibility to discover that path. And here is the truth we so easily forget: *It will look different for every individual.*

God simply is not into cookie cutters. He does not mass-produce human beings. He creates countless stars of different sizes, brightness, colors, and mass and calls each one by its own name. He leads everyone on their own path, and even that individual path may look different at various times and in various locations. There simply is no one-size-fits-all divine directive on how a believer is to use the wealth entrusted to him or her. God remains sovereign over His gifts of wealth, just as He remains sovereign over all His other gifts. What applies, then, to spiritual gifts applies equally to God's financial gifts:

"All these are the work of one and the same Spirit, and He gives them to each one, just as He determines" (1 Corinthians 12:11).

It took me quite some time to make this discovery.

Follow Me!

Many years ago, I erred badly in thinking that Jesus intended the account of the rich young ruler to be a universal principle applicable to every believer. I have learned through the years that although God calls each believing, baptized Christian to reflect His own generosity in their giving choices and lifestyle, the manner in which they do so may (and probably will) look very different from person to person.

If you are looking for a single standard to guide you, I can't help you. I cannot direct you to one universal yardstick spelled out in percentages or laws. The only divine standard I know of requires each child of God to discover the unique standard that the Lord reveals to each of His children. The truth is that *God leads in ways specific to each individual.*

At the end of the Gospel of John, after the resurrected Christ appears to His disciples and gives them breakfast by the sea, Jesus and Peter go for a walk. Jesus restores the apostle after Peter denied three times that he even knew his Lord, and then he gives Peter a prophecy of the kind of death he will suffer to "glorify God." Finally Jesus says to Peter, "Follow me!"

The prophecy clearly rattles the apostle. As he looks around, he sees John, "the disciple whom Jesus loved," following them. And so he turns to Jesus, perhaps points to John, and says, "Lord, what about *him*?"

Jesus immediately replies, "If I want him to remain alive until I return, what is that to you? You must follow me" (John 21:19–22).

Peter apparently wanted to know if the standard Jesus had just given to him would apply equally to John. And Jesus tells him frankly, in essence, "That's none of your business. How I lead John has nothing to do with how I lead you. If I ask the two of you to walk very different paths, that's my business. Your business is to follow me wherever I lead."

> *If you're still on the journey to discovering God's purposes for your wealth, don't give up. Keep going. He'll show you what you need to know, in His own time.*

This account seems to be reflected in a wonderful passage in *The Horse and His Boy*, the fifth book in C. S. Lewis's Chronicles of Narnia series. Aslan, the Christ figure in the books, is explaining to Shasta, the boy of the title, how his recent adventures—even the terrifying ones—were all designed to bring him to this place in the story. Aslan explains,

> "I was the lion who forced you to join with Aravis. I was the cat who comforted you among the houses of the dead. I was the lion who drove the jackals

from you while you slept. I was the lion who gave the Horses the new strength of fear for the last mile so that you should reach King Lune in time. And I was the lion you do not remember who pushed the boat in which you lay, a child near death, so that it came to shore where a man sat, wakeful at midnight, to receive you."

"Then it was you who wounded Aravis?"

"It was I."

"But what for?"

"Child," said the Voice, "I am telling you your story, not hers. I tell no one any story but his own."

While we can gain insight by looking at the stories of others, we will find no blueprints for our own houses there, no treasure maps to guide us to our own inheritance. Your story is your own, and God writes unique plot twists and unexpected character arcs into each story He directs.

Different Stories, Different Paths

Many factors can contribute to the disparity we see in the distinctive ways God leads us on our individual paths. Let me mention just three of them.

Maturity of faith. God does not lead and guide children in the same way that He leads and guides mature adults, any more than a kindergarten teacher instructs her pupils in the same way that a university professor guides her PhD students.

If you recently came to faith in Jesus, He may well lead you along a different path than the one you see a seasoned believer walking. And the path He has you walk in ten years likely will not look exactly the same as the one you're on now. "When I was a child," Paul writes, "I talked like a child, I thought like a child, I reasoned like a child. When I became a man, I put childish ways behind me" (1 Corinthians 13:11). The same principle holds here.

Changing seasons of life. Maybe you've known Jesus since you were five years old. Maybe you grew up in Him and became mature in your midtwenties. But now you're in midlife, or perhaps approaching retirement age. Jesus often leads us in different ways at different seasons of life, not because we reach some new level of maturity, but because that's just what He does. The apostle John wrote to the members of a much-loved church, frequently addressing various individuals as "dear children," "fathers," and "young men." At various seasons of life, we need various kinds of guidance. The same is true in how we manage our wealth.

Still on the journey to discovering God's purposes for your wealth. It took Susie and me a long time to begin to discover God's purposes for the wealth He entrusted to us, and we're still learning. And I'm a pastor! If you're still on the journey to discovering God's purposes for your wealth, don't give up. Keep going. He'll show you what you need to know, in His own time. I know this because He promises it: "Trust in the LORD with all your heart, and lean not on your own understanding; in all your ways acknowledge Him, and He shall direct your paths" (Proverbs 3:5–6, NKJV). That includes the path He wants you to walk with your wealth.

Always Becoming, Never Arriving

Whatever the reason for the discrepancy in how Christians live with their wealth, we must never forget that none of us, in this life, ever fully comes to the end of our journey.

We are *always* becoming, we *never* arrive.

I like the honest, up-front way Paul put it to his friends in Philippi: "Yet, my brothers, I do not consider myself to have 'arrived,' spiritually, nor do I consider myself already perfect. But I keep going on, grasping ever more firmly that purpose for which Christ grasped me" (Philippians 3:12, Phillips).

When a person first surrenders his life to Jesus as Lord, is that surrender ever fully complete? No. Within each disciple of Christ, there are secreted areas of life that the Spirit of God has not yet redeemed. Why? One reason is that we so cherish those areas that we don't want the Lord to rule over them. Another is that God sanctifies us through a lifelong process.

Imagine what would happen if Christ entered a man's life and suddenly revealed to him everything erroneous and false. He would implode from the weight of such knowledge! Christ's manner is to reveal piece by piece, step by step, throughout a lifetime, all that must come under His Lordship and grace... including the stewardship of our wealth.

This pilgrimage, this journey, always begins with a single step. What's the one step God may be telling you to take right now that you need to surrender to Him and say, "Lord, this is yours. How do I use it for you?"

18

STUFF HAPPENS

M any Christians of capacity struggle for years with the idea of "God's will." First, we wrestle with the very notion of freely submitting to God's will and seeking to co-operate with Him in whatever *He* wants to accomplish in and through our lives. That struggle itself can feel utterly exhausting. But it's only half the battle.

When at last we experience the deep joy found only in embracing God's will as our own, not long afterward we run into a different kind of struggle. Surprisingly, this one can feel every bit as exhausting as the first one. It often goes something like this:

"Lord, I'm ready for whatever You call me to do. But how do I discover what You have in mind? I'm willing and eager to do Your will... *but what is it?*"

What Should I Do?

Elsewhere I've suggested that all of us need to go through a process of discovery to find out where God may be calling us to serve Him and how we can best use the resources He's entrusted to us. Here I'd like to focus a little more on the theological aspects of that process.

How is God's Spirit involved? Should we expect to get visions in the night, hear an audible voice calling out instructions, find a treasure map with "X marks the spot"?

One good way to get our biblical bearings might be to investigate how the Spirit led the very first Christians, as described in the book of Acts. One of the biggest things I'd like us to grasp is that, if you look beyond some of the particulars of God's leading, you start to see one very important and consistent pattern. And if we can grab hold of that, it can do more to give us confidence and encouragement in "doing God's will" than almost anything else I know.

But I have to tell you, it may not look much like what you expect!

> *God typically leads His people by sending them someplace or positioning them someplace, and then "stuff happens." He doesn't tend to give them detailed instructions or complete mission briefs.*

Let's begin with Philip, one of the seven men chosen by the apostles to help take care of the church's physical needs. Philip was just a guy, not an apostle or a prophet or anything like that. Luke, the author of Acts, describes him as "full of the Spirit and wisdom" (Acts 6:3).

When a huge persecution breaks out against Christians in Jerusalem and a large number of believers scatter to the four winds, Philip takes off for a large city called Samaria (its ruins lie in the mountains of the West Bank near a Palestinian city named Sebastia). A great revival breaks out there, bringing "great joy" to the city (Acts 8:8).

But then something unusual happens.

At the height of all the excitement, an angel tells Philip, "Go out to the road—the desert road—that goes down from Jerusalem to Gaza" (Acts 8:26). That's it. No other instructions. No great vision, no detailed battle plans. Just, "Hoof it out to the dusty, desert road."

It would have been like Billy Graham getting called away in the middle of a great New York City Crusade and told to go out to a country road near Pompton Lakes, New Jersey. It didn't appear to make much sense... but Philip takes his leave of the Greater Samaria Crusade and starts walking.

When he finally reaches the designated road, he sees a man in a chariot reading the book of Isaiah. This time the Spirit (not an angel) tells Philip, "Go to that chariot and stay near it" (8:29). And that's it. Nothing else. He gets no other instructions. Just, "See that guy? Go stand in his vicinity."

Oh, but what an amazing encounter it turns out to be! The man, a wealthy official from an important African kingdom, becomes the first convert from (and missionary to!) Africa. And all because Philip acts on the first, small divine direction he gets: "Walk down this desert road."

This little story encapsulates for me how God often leads. I don't mean that you should expect to see an angel (although I suppose you could; I never have) or hear an audible word from God (Luke doesn't tell us how the Spirit spoke to Philip). God typically leads His people by sending them someplace or positioning them someplace, and then "stuff happens." He doesn't tend to give them detailed instructions or complete mission briefs. He just says, in one way or another, "Go here," and then *stuff happens.*

One story does not a pattern make. But similar things take place, in different ways, all through the book of Acts.

Consider the conversion of Saul. After Jesus knocks him off his horse with a blinding light (by the way, this single incident ought to dispel the notion of a gentle Jesus who would never *dream* of getting rough with those He wants to use), He told the dazed and confused apostle-to-be, "Now get up and go into the city, and you will be told what you must do" (Acts 9:6). Not so much as a "pardon me"! Just, "Get up, go in, and wait."

Years later, when the apostle Paul recounts this story, he adds a little detail about the Lord's words to him. When Saul asks, "What shall I do, Lord?" Jesus answers him, "Get up and go into Damascus. There you will be told *all that you have been assigned to do*" (Acts 22:10, italics added). While Saul gets a thumbnail picture of what is to come, he gets no real details. But I like the description about his assignment. Paul had a divine assignment. You have one, too. So do I. It won't be given to us on a silver platter. It won't get downloaded onto our iPad. It probably won't be revealed all at once. But once we take the first step, God will reveal the second. And the third. And the fourth. Throughout a lifetime.

In Acts, a lot of this divine leading appears to happen quickly. But that's a little misleading. Shortly after Saul comes to faith in Christ, for example, the church sends him back to his hometown of Tarsus so his infuriated enemies don't kill him. We're not told how long he stays there; I've seen expert guesses at anywhere from a couple of years to a dozen. Saul disappears from Acts in 9:30 and doesn't show up again until 11:25. What does he do all that time? Does he plead for God to lead him and yet remain stuck in his hometown? He has no idea that one day he'll be the apostle Paul (the name change isn't recorded until Acts 13:9), the author of half of the New Testament.

God had to prepare Saul for his challenging road ahead—and the Lord tends to do a lot of such preparation in the background, in the backwaters of life where nothing much seems to be happening and everything seems to have stalled. Saul has to wait there in Tarsus until his friend Barnabas comes down to look for him so he can take him up to the big leagues. The pair then works together for a whole year in Antioch (incidentally, but not coincidentally, the place where the followers of Jesus are first called Christians, in Acts 11:26).

But even two or three stories do not a good pattern make. So what about Peter? Just before God opens up membership in the church to Jews *and* Gentiles, the Spirit gives Peter a perplexing set of experiences. The apostle sits there, puzzled, and then the Spirit tells him, "Simon, three men are looking for you. So get up and go downstairs. Do not hesitate to go with them, for I have sent them" (10:19, 20). Again, nothing else. No other instructions. No hint at the convulsive changes about to hit. Just, "Get up and go."

Oh, and neither does God explain the weird experiences until Peter "got up and went" and found himself in unfamiliar territory where "stuff happened." Only then did it all start to make sense.

But none of it ever would have made sense, and in fact none of it even would have *happened*, unless Peter had followed the tiny bit of divine leading he got: "Get up and go."

After Barnabas and Saul prove themselves as effective workers in Antioch, the Spirit says *to the church* (not to the individuals), "Set apart for me Barnabas and Saul for the work to which I have called them" (Acts 13:2). What work? Not explained. How to pay for it? Unclear. "Set apart" means, basically, "move them into position." And so the church's first great missionary journeys get ready to launch.

Sometime later, Paul and his missionary band run into a little trouble. They prayerfully make plans to visit one area, but things don't work out. They make new plans to visit someplace else, but "the Spirit of Jesus would not allow them to" (Acts 16:7). So they keep moving. One night, probably after another frustrating day, Paul has a dream in which a Macedonian man says to him, "Come over to Macedonia and help us" (Acts 16:9). Paul and his friends talk it over the next day and "conclude" that God has called them to preach in Macedonia. They make straight for the target area and soon start talking to a woman, not a man (as in the dream), and she becomes the first believer in Europe.

And so it goes.

Stuff Still Happens

Throughout Acts, the same pattern continues. Over and over and over again.

So I'd recommend that if *you* want to do God's will, look for the smallest divine leading you can detect. It'll often be something like, "Get up and go here." And then watch as "stuff happens."

19

THE APPLE ORCHARD

My great brother and mentor, Ray Lyne, once gave me a potent metaphor for understanding biblical stewardship.

Imagine you own an apple orchard that you want to use to invest in kingdom causes. You have two apparent options (I will show a third way later).

The first option is to give a tithe of the profits you make each year from the sale of your apples. This approach may not allow you to maximize your ability to invest, but it will provide a steady stream of kingdom dollars for years to come.

Second, you could sell all the apples, cut down all the trees and sell them for firewood, and then sell off all the land. The sum from all three would be exponentially greater than merely giving a portion from the sale of apples.

Wow, what a great and powerful witness that would be!

At least, for a while.

But then... what would you have to give the following year, and the year after that, and the year after that? When you cut down all the trees, there are no more apples. And if you no longer had anything to manage, would you still be a steward of God?

Ray's story gave me pause as I contemplated what Susie and I should do with the money generated by her family's estate. As I've said, my natural inclination was to sell it all and give it all away. But would that make me a good steward... or simply a onetime auctioneer?

A Place at the Table

As we discussed how to best proceed, I remember hearing a story of a businessman who initiated a strategy similar to what I had been contemplating. He sold his business, but instead of warehousing a significant portion in a donor-advised fund at NCF or some other private foundation, he wanted all his kingdom-directed dollars to have immediate impact. Therefore he gave away $8 million to five or six ministries that he loved and trusted. Most of those ministries received seven-figure gifts.

Suddenly, he got moved from being just a good friend of the ministries to a "mega-ministry partner." He got invited to serve on some very prominent boards. He was now a kingdom player!

But the following year, since his income had drastically shrunk, his contributions also diminished significantly. And so the super-mega-ministry partner of one year before became once again just the good friend of the ministry. To his surprise, after his board terms ended, some of the ministries didn't ask him to return. Oh, he continued to be generous with what he had, but it wasn't enough to warrant him a place at the table.

So did the man do something wrong? Not necessarily. If he

believed God wanted him to do what he did, then I believe he did the right thing.

Of course, I'm not saying that the ministries behaved righteously in dropping the man from their boards. But what might have happened had he chosen another route to steward the wealth the Lord had given him?

Give and Hold

From the late '90s, when I felt the urge to sell Susie's interest in the family business and so increase our kingdom impact (and, not coincidentally, impress my Christian friends), to this very day, a very wonderful thing has transpired. The value of Susie's family business interest has more than doubled while the size of our distributions (the amount of money generated by selling the apples) has tripled. In hindsight, I now realize that our ability to exercise a sizable kingdom impact from just managing Susie's "apple orchard" has *far* exceeded what we could have accomplished if we had sold out years earlier.

The third way I mentioned earlier is an extension of the approach we took. In essence, it blends the two main giving strategies described at the beginning of this chapter. It is called Give and Hold.

Give and Hold is a unique and wonderful tool for Christian businessmen, developed by the National Christian Foundation, to enable them to divest of a portion of their business interest so they can enhance their kingdom impact, while not compromising their ability to run their businesses. And it does so even as it reduces both income taxes and capital gains taxes.

Very simply, business people donate nonvoting shares of a business to the National Christian Foundation, which provides an immediate tax deduction for the full appraised value of the shares. It could be held in C or S corporations (stock), a general partnership, or a limited liability company (LLC) or partnership (LLP). Though NCF holds the legal ownership of the donated portion, voting rights of the donated shares remain with the donor. Then each time the company makes a distribution, the portion of the donated interest/share goes to NCF, which it puts in the giving fund set up by the business donor. Those proceeds are his or hers (or a family's) to give to whatever kingdom charities they love most. If and when the final sale of the business ever takes place, that portion of the donated asset goes into the donor's giving fund, eliminating all capital gains on that portion.

The great thing about the National Christian Foundation is that it allows you to warehouse your resources until you figure out how God wants you to utilize them. And so you commit a portion of your resources to God now, while waiting for Him to reveal more of His plan to you. It permits you to engage in a period of probing and exploring to see what God has really put on your heart.

> *In hindsight, I now realize that our ability to exercise a sizable kingdom impact from just managing Susie's "apple orchard" has far exceeded what we could have accomplished if we had sold out years earlier.*

Shrinking a Big Net

Because in the beginning Susie and I had only a general sense of what we would like to invest in, we used a really big net to find the right kingdom opportunities. But that big net helped us to determine what really excited us, what God had put on our hearts. We started to gradually reduce the size of the net, becoming more focused in our giving. And so we maximized our kingdom impact.

Such a giving path does not differ much from trying to determine God's calling on your life. I like a quotation attributed to Michelangelo. When an observer asked the famous artist, "How did you sculpt such a perfect *David*?" He responded, "I kept chipping away that which wasn't *David*."

Finding out how God unleashes passion and purpose in your life involves a process of discovery. In fact, it's something we ought to do throughout our lives. Why? Because God is always on the move; His work is never static. *Harvard Business Review* calls this "discovery-driven planning." You start with a general idea of where you want to go and what you want to do, but you continually test your assumptions and question your strategies.

To put it more biblically, "In his heart a man plans his course, but the LORD determines his steps" (Proverbs 16:9). God can't steer a boat tied to the dock, but that doesn't mean we launch prematurely into the great blue, without a clue where we're going. If you have no clear sense of direction, then pray and probe until something becomes clearer.

One day my foundation board asked me to identify a region in the world where we as a foundation could invest long and deep, knowing that if we were to have any meaningful impact, we must remain committed there for a long period of time. I visited five countries, and after each visit, I wanted to choose that country… until I visited the next country. My dilemma echoed Proverbs 18:17: "The first to present his case seems right, till another comes forward and questions him."

Finally, we decided on the Philippines, and more specifically, the underserved island of Mindanao. We have worked there for ten years now and have a team in place that not only monitors our grants but also provides meaningful friendship and coaching to those who live and work on the front lines.

Last year, we launched a new training and coaching program with Mission Increase Foundation. When we did the official launch in 2014, all the groups we invited showed up to hear about the new ministry, designed to assist them in building their organizational capacity. We got a tremendous response, in large part because our foundation sponsored it; we were no longer just some new kid on the block but had shown ourselves to be faithful and trustworthy for many years. We never would have gotten there, however, if Susie and I had not held on to the apple orchard.

What If?

While I always wanted to be faithful to God, I also wanted to live in a way that inspired others to live generously before God, just as others had inspired me. So I played the what-if game.

What if Susie sold out her interest in the family businesses and we donated half of it to our giving fund at the National

Christian Foundation and took another portion to form a charitable remainder trust to help offset our loss of income? It made perfect and holy sense to me.

Only one big problem: it wasn't mine to give. It was my wife's, and she would *never* want to do something like this, because she owned part of a family legacy—her Tara, as she often referred to it.

As they say in sports, sometimes the best trades are the ones that never get made. By holding onto our orchard, we have given away far more than we would have had we tried to sell it so many years ago.

20

BLESSED TO BE A BLESSING

The whole world loved the *Toy Story* movies. All three films (so far—another is slated for 2018) set box office records, together grossing almost $2 *billion*. We apparently can't resist the idea of inanimate toys coming to life and having secret adventures of their own. What would my own childhood toys say, I wonder, if they could talk?

But why limit it to toys? What might other inanimate objects say if they suddenly came to life? I wonder if the following items would say anything like this when...

A car got filled up with gas: *"That feels so satisfying!"*

A grocery bag overflowed with groceries: *"If I had a belt, I'd have to loosen it."*

A wallet got stuffed with cash? *"Look out, ladies, Big Daddy's in town!"*

A cell phone was fully recharged? *"I'm so energized, I'm absolutely electrifying!"*

But then take it a little further. What would happen if you tried to use one of these contented items to serve you as its designers intended? What might the car say, for example, if you tried to take it on a family vacation?

> *"Stop! I'm full, and you want to empty my tank? Take a hike, tubby!"*

What if you started removing your groceries from the bag to make an evening meal?

> *"Hey, you! Step away from the food and keep your filthy hands to yourself!"*

What if you tried to grab a twenty dollar bill from your billfold?

> *"Who do you think you are, sticky fingers? That's mine!"*

What if you picked up your cell phone to call your best friend for a long, overdue conversation?

> *"I didn't get charged up all night just so you could blab my life away!"*

Ridiculous, right? We don't build cars just to fill their tanks. We design grocery bags to transport groceries, not to give food a permanent home. Wallets provide only temporary accommodations for money and cell phones exist to help us keep in touch with the outside world. We bless these things with gas, food, money, and electricity *so that* they can bless us by fulfilling their designed function. A car that wants to stay full and not go anywhere has missed its purpose in life.

I wonder... do you think men and women who want to hoard blessings but never give them out may have missed their life purpose, too?

A Rainbow in Someone Else's Cloud

When you bless others, you become a conductor of happiness. "The thing to do, it seems to me," said Maya Angelou, "is to prepare yourself so you can be a rainbow in somebody else's cloud."

Are you a rainbow in anybody else's cloud?

The Bible insists that God blesses His people *so that* they may bless others. The apostle Paul wrote, "You will be made rich in every way, *so that* you can be generous on every occasion" (2 Corinthians 9:11, italics added). God does not bless us merely to make it possible to replace an old Timex with a new Rolex. He blesses us so we can use some of the resources He provides us to generously supply the needs of others, resulting in multiple expressions of "thanksgiving to God" (verse 11).

We are blessed to be a blessing.

"A generous man will prosper," says Proverbs 11:25; "he who refreshes others will himself be refreshed." God comforts us "in all our troubles," Paul tells us, "so that we can comfort those in any trouble with the comfort we ourselves have received from God" (2 Corinthians 1:4).

Again, blessed to be a blessing.

> *On a scale of one to ten, how would*
> *you rate yourself in utilizing* all *your*
> *wealth to be a blessing to God*
> *and your neighbor?*

Imagine an accountant's ledger. On one side of the ledger is a column marked *Mine*. That can contain anything in my life that I hold on to, anything that I refuse to allow God to use to bless others. I simply make it off-limits to God. It may be my business, my hobbies, my bank account, my relationships, my lifestyle.

On the other side of the ledger is a column marked *God's*. These are the areas of life that I have allowed the light of God's Spirit to penetrate, which I offer to Him to use as He desires.

On a scale of one to ten, how would you rate yourself in utilizing *all* your wealth to be a blessing to God and your neighbor? How are you doing? Do you find yourself saying something like, "Oh, I am great in giving time," or, "I'm great with financial gifts," but never really giving much thought to the others? I'd guess that describes most of us.

It did not, however, describe Abraham, whose children we're supposed to be.

Abraham's Blessing

God says to Abraham in Genesis 12:2, "I will make you into a great nation and I will bless you; I will make your name great, and you will be a blessing." Notice five things.

First, to whom does God speak these words? To Abraham, the father of our faith. And if it holds true for the father, then does it not also apply to his children, the children of faith?

Second, when did God speak these words to Abraham? The Lord made this part of His new relationship with Abraham right from the very start. This is the very first thing in the scriptural record that God says to Abraham. It is the foundation of his calling by God. It is not some afterthought, hastily added later in a moment of reflection. No, what we have here is a preamble that lays down the terms of God's covenant relationship with Abraham. It describes in brief a life lived by faith in God.

Third, who is the source and author of Abraham's wealth and blessings? That's easy: God. First Chronicles 29:12 tells us that both "wealth and honor" come from God. He is the giver of *good* things, not *evil* things: "Every good gift and every perfect gift is from above, coming down from the Father of lights with whom there is no variation or shadow due to change" (James 1:17, ESV). Wealth does not have to corrupt its stewards; if it did, then we would believe in a sadistic God, no better than the devil, who lures us with pleasure and treasure only to destroy us through use of the gift.

Fourth, wealth is more than just money. God promised to give Abraham *everything* he needed to become a great nation: land, people, even the intangible things we value so much, like a good name. Likewise, God's blessing to us includes everything God gives us: our possessions, whether land, house, stocks, and cars, or whether our good name, our talents, and our abilities. *All* come from Him. Our wealth includes everything we have and everything we are.

Fifth, God invested in Abraham for a purpose. The Lord tells Abraham, "I will bless you so that you can hoard my blessings to yourself." Really? No, not really. God blessed Abraham so that he would "be a blessing."

A blessing… to whom?

The statement is left open-ended. And how was He to bless these unspecified individuals? Not with *some* of His blessings, but with *all* God had given him. God did not give Abraham the option to pick and choose what part of his wealth he would use to bless others. God never intended this to be a multiple-choice question. I often hear people say, "I don't have to give money, I give my time," or, "I don't have to use my talents or abilities for God—I give my money." But God did not ask Abraham (or any of us) to use only part of his wealth to bless others. Abraham had a responsibility, and so do we, to use it *all*—time, talent, possessions, finances, skills, the whole enchilada.

Abraham accepted this charge from God and today we remember him for blessing his world. Will our world remember us, as Abraham's children, for blessing it?

Acting Like Abraham's Children

A few years ago, Susie and I attended a twenty-fifth anniversary celebration at a church where I had pastored. The emcee was a real jokester, but also a friend. Part of the service recalled the ministries of each of the church's pastors.

When the emcee got to me, he said, "Isn't it great to have the Perrys back in the church?" He immediately pulled out a checkbook and waved it in the air. "We've missed you!" he said.

While Susie didn't much care for his brand of humor, I tried to accept his little joke in the spirit in which he offered it. He didn't mean to say they missed us only because we no longer contributed some of our resources to the ministry. Rather, he meant it as a thanks for our willingness to use our resources to bless others through the church. I took his comments as a reminder of our great privilege to act like Abraham's children, as described in the chorus of Scott Wesley Brown's song "Blessed to Be a Blessing":

> We've been blessed to be a blessing
> We've been loved to give His love
> Made mighty so we can fulfill His call
> We've been blessed to be a blessing
> With enough to give enough
> For the greatest in His kingdom
> Is the servant of us all.

21

BE GRATEFUL FOR THE GIFT

For days, fear had gripped Benjamin's heart. They'd all heard the reports: a huge invading army had sailed across the sea and even now was marching toward Jerusalem. The alarmed king had called a fast for the entire country and led a public prayer for mercy at the temple. "We do not know what to do," he had prayed, "but our eyes are upon you."

A Levite had stood up and loudly prophesied that God would save his people; they would not have to lift a sword or fire an arrow. But they *would* have to go out to the battlefield and watch God do His work.

While Benjamin felt better after that, worry again engulfed him today. Early this morning, as his countrymen had set out for the Desert of Tekoa, the king appointed a few men to move to the head of the line to sing praises to God—*and Benjamin was one of them!* Despite his great fear, he took courage as he saw the faith of his friends and so joined them in song:

> Give thanks to the Lord,
> For His love endures forever!

Soon Benjamin and the others at the head of the line saw their enemies spread out before them, like a swarm of hungry locusts covering the land. Just as the terror began welling up in his heart once again, something odd and glorious happened: the mighty attacking armies started to attack... *themselves*! By the time the Hebrews reached their enemies, they found nothing but corpses littering the landscape, as far as the eye could see.

Three days later, the whole nation of Judah assembled in the valley where the miracle had taken place. There they gave thanks and praised their God. Someone named the site the Valley of Praise. The name stuck, obviously.

> Benjamin felt only too happy to give thanks to his God for such an unexpected gift. (Based on 2 Chronicles 20:1–30.)

Gratitude for the Gift of Wealth

Praise and thanksgiving is the missing jewel in the crown of many Christians of capacity. While gratitude is the seed from which all other virtues grow, in order for us to be virtuous with our wealth, we must begin with an attitude of gratitude. Unfortunately, I doubt that all Christians of capacity feel the gratitude required to liberate them to a life of generosity.

Like the fictional Benjamin above, they let fear rob them of the confidence and faith God wants them to have as they seek to wisely use the wealth He's entrusted to them. What do they fear? They fear what others may think. They fear they may not be doing enough. They fear they may support the wrong project. They fear they may have to walk a path—at the front of the line?—for which they feel ill equipped.

> *Have you consecrated your wealth for God's*
> *use? Have you sanctified it and set it apart*
> *for Him to use as He directs? Until you*
> *do that, it will be hard for you to give God*
> *wholehearted thanks for His gift.*

But most of all, perhaps, they fear that their wealth is somehow tainted, maybe a little unholy, something to feel guilty or ashamed about. And how can they celebrate and be generous with something that they fear may not even belong in the kingdom of God?

I've learned that Christians of capacity can celebrate what they have and be generous with it only when they begin to embrace the truth that *God* has given them everything they own.

As we saw in chapter fifteen, God does not give wealth universally. He sovereignly chooses who gets what gift—and who are we to diminish or feel embarrassed by whatever gift God gives us? We can fully embrace it only with thanksgiving. Wholehearted giving of thanks enables us to fully value it for what it is, a gift from God. Without that, we can't fully use it to accomplish the purposes God has in mind.

Moving from Guilt to Gratitude

I know many of us find it hard to move from no gratitude to deep gratitude. Sometimes it takes more than knowing God is the giver of wealth to get to the right place. So how can we become people of thanksgiving for *everything* God brings into our lives, including our wealth?

The first step to receiving our wealth as a sacred gift is to thank God for it, whatever we may feel at the time:

> For everything God created is good, and nothing is to be rejected if it is received with thanksgiving, because it is consecrated by the word of God and prayer. (1 Timothy 4:4, 5)

God says He creates wealth. Since Paul labels "everything God created" as "good," that good includes your wealth. But the apostle goes beyond that. He tells us that *nothing* God created is to be "rejected," so long as it is "received with thanksgiving."

So let me ask: Have you rejected in some way the wealth God has given you? Do you feel embarrassed by it, guilty for having it, compelled to hide it? Paul would tell you, "Listen, you can never fully enjoy or use the good gifts God gives to you unless you receive them with thanksgiving. That includes your wealth."

If we can celebrate our Creator's handiwork in magnificent natural settings—the thunder of a great waterfall or shimmer of moonlight on a calm sea—can't we also rejoice in the beauty of the things the Lord's people create through the use of their God-given gifts? Can't we also celebrate the beauty of what our wealth can generate in service to our King? When we give thanks for these things, we release the full power of the gift.

Paul reminds us that these gifts must be "consecrated." To consecrate something is to sanctify it, to make it holy, to set it apart for God's use.

Have you consecrated your wealth for God's use? Have you sanctified it and set it apart for Him to use as He directs? Until you do that, it will be hard for you to give God wholehearted thanks for His gift.

Paul adds that we "consecrate" these gifts by "the word of God and prayer." That is, whatever we do with these gifts must line up with God's purposes as described in the Bible, which enables us to pray about them with confidence. As we read and study God's Word, we become more and more familiar with His heart—and so we get a better and better sense of how we can use the wealth He gives us to benefit others, enjoy ourselves, and glorify Him. And as we pray about the ventures we believe we need to undertake, He guides and directs us, which prompts us to thank Him all the more for His goodness.

The Power of Giving Thanks

Christians of capacity are *Christians*, first and foremost, and so the directive given to all believers applies equally to them: "Give thanks in all circumstances, for this is God's will for you in Christ Jesus" (1 Thessalonians 5:18). If you're seeking God's will for how you can best use your wealth, this is a great place to begin. His will is that you give Him thanks for what He has given you. When you start from that base, good things tend to happen.

This holds true even when *bad* things happen. When Susie

and I suffered a series of miscarriages many years ago, I discovered the value and purpose of saying, "Thank you, Lord," not *for* what happened, but *in* what happened.

Martin Luther likened our relationship with Christ to a marriage. All that is mine is His, and all that is His is mine. Surely I can always be thankful for that? He gets my sin and my broken life, but also my gifts, abilities, and possessions. In return, I get His righteousness. But far more than that, I get *Him*.

That sounds something like my marriage to Susie! When we got married, she got my college debt, my eleven-year-old car, and me. (Who said life was fair?) And I got her growing bank account, her two-year-old car, and *her*. How could I not "give thanks in all circumstances"?

Giving thanks also serves as a pressure valve when things get difficult. I have a friend who a few years ago went through a very dark time, even spending a couple of weeks at the hospital, diagnosed with acute anxiety and clinical depression. He prayed a lot before the worst of it hit, but today he thinks he left out a key item. He missed part of what Paul wrote:

> Do not be anxious about anything, but in everything, by prayer and petition, *with thanksgiving*, present your requests to God. And the peace of God, which transcends all understanding, will guard your hearts and your minds in Christ Jesus (Philippians 4:6–7, emphasis added).

Although my friend prayed continually about his challenging circumstances, without applying the thanksgiving part of Paul's admonition, his prayers tended to focus his attention on the problems confronting him rather than on the God who had always proved faithful in the past. He believes that omission played a significant role in his crash. You needn't let that happen to you.

Let Gratitude Blossom

Gratitude can't fully blossom in our lives until we begin to grasp the grace and freedom that God gives us with our wealth. He wants us to enjoy it. He wants us to use it for His purposes. And He wants us to thank Him for His gift.

So let's join Paul: "Thanks be to God for His indescribable gift!" (2 Corinthians 9:15).

22

RICH IN GOOD DEEDS

When the apostle Paul instructed Timothy to command Christians of capacity in his church "to be rich in good deeds, and to be generous and willing to share" (1 Timothy 6:18), I expect he had in mind all kinds of creative deeds. As I ponder that command for myself, I often consider two aspects of Christian wealth that I believe can help to prompt positive change in our society.

Gospel Patronage

The first comes from a recent book titled *Gospel Patrons: People Whose Generosity Changed the World*. The book chronicles the role played by wealthy believers in empowering great movements of God through the years, initiatives that often altered the face of the planet.

The heroes and heroines depicted are not current figures; they all lived prior to the twentieth century. *Gospel Patrons* contends that many great historical characters—Tyndale, Wilberforce, Whitefield, Newton, and others, godly leaders who sparked enormous and positive change in their world in the name of their God—would not have succeeded without the wealthy benefactors who believed in their call and in their vision to make a difference.

The author, John Rinehart, gave me a signed copy of his book along with the inscription, "Thanks for your help and encouragement along the way. I hope this book strengthens you for your own sense of calling and stewardship." Indeed it has.

Gospel patronage, however, can take some funny turns. For example, one of the best grants we ever offered was one we never made.

> *It's not wrong to lay up treasure for yourself! But you do so not by hanging on to every last penny, but by seeking ways to "be rich in good deeds."*

We got involved with an organization called Free Wheelchair Mission almost from its inception, when it began as an alpha fund at the NCF Southern California office. Since it didn't yet have its tax-exempt status, we took it under our umbrella until it got the requisite paperwork completed. The mission began in 2001 and since then has given away more than nine hundred thousand wheelchairs.

Around 2004 or 2005, the organization had just started to gain some traction and recognition within the church community. Susie and I had lunch one September day with the founder and his wife, Don and Laurie Schoendorfer. They had just begun planning their first Christmas appeal, hoping to raise about $400,000 to order new chairs. But they had a problem.

In order to have the chairs ready for Christmas delivery, they had to order them in September. But if they ordered them then and didn't raise all the money they needed, they'd find themselves in a very deep hole.

"Well, Don," I said, "I'll tell you what we'll do. Susie and I will cover whatever you're short. So go ahead and put in your order."

We didn't end up having to pay a dime, because the ministry raised all the funds it needed, and then some. But our offer enabled our friends to move ahead. That's the power of gospel patronage.

Rekindling an Old Partnership

The second thought stems from a vision that I believe God gave me a year and a half ago. I want to do what I can to help re-create the reality that used to exist in the US (and still does in other parts of the world) where the civic, corporate, and church sectors work together for the benefit of the common good of their communities. Let me give one example of what I mean.

Back in the 1990s a group of passionate Christians decided to reach into the barrios of Orange County. The outreach began in a very small way, utilizing a couple of apartments for after-school programs, mentoring and summer Vacation Bible School–style outreaches. About ten years after the ministry began, a group of well-meaning business people got behind the organization and helped move its primary operations into a ten-thousand-square-foot community center. In no time at all, the ministry became a darling of the corporate community, supported by many major corporations.

Although the mission of the organization never changed, its communication regarding its mission and vision did, to the point that the spiritual emphasis of its holistic ministry got de-emphasized. Part of the problem resulted from a board expansion designed to create more places at the table for corporate supporters, individuals who valued the group's educational efforts but who may never have fully understood its spiritual foundation.

At one point, the ministry wanted to double its size by acquiring an adjacent building, so it set out to do a feasibility study. That study revealed confusion among the ministry's supporters, especially in regard to the group's holistic purpose and mission.

When the organization approached us to participate in a capital campaign to buy the expanded facilities, I had some very serious conversations with staff members about the group's mission and vision. I figured that if we were to have any influence in helping to solidify who and what this ministry represented, we needed to step up big-time with a challenge grant. But for us to make the grant, the board had to agree to our memorandum of understanding (MOU), which affirmed the group's spiritual foundation, stipulated that its new executive director had to buy in completely to its holistic ministry, and addressed a few other organizational items.

To our great delight, the board expressed complete agreement with our MOU. And to my surprise, I found the board had never been contentious about the spiritual foundations of the ministry; its members simply assumed it and never gave it the importance it deserved. Our condition regarding the executive director was a no-brainer and they already had begun working on the organizational changes that would ensure a successful future for the ministry.

My point here—and this may help to explain why the YMCA, the Red Cross, Harvard University, and other high-profile groups lost their spiritual footing through the years—is not that such groups inevitably get hijacked by forces malicious to the Gospel. Rather, they slowly drift away from their moorings as they pursue the friendship of wealthy patrons in the corporate world who value their work but may not share or value their spiritual underpinnings. Peter Greer's book *Mission Drift* offers some valuable insight into this process.

What might have happened in these organizations, however, if wealthy Christians had continued their generous support while holding firm to the original vision and mission of the various groups? The mission drift we've witnessed repeatedly might never have taken place.

The reality is that, more often than not, gold rules. Funding becomes the guiding light for many Christian organizations that do a good work in their communities, because funds are always scarce and the needs never ending. If we hope and pray that these ministries don't lose sight of their spiritual values, and if we Christians truly want a voice at the table where the church intersects with the civic and corporate worlds, then we can't just insist on sharing our ideals, as important as they are. We must include our wealth as well, because in the end, money usually trumps good intentions.

Lay Up Treasure

Paul didn't instruct Timothy merely to command the wealthy to be rich in good deeds. He also wanted him to remind these Christians of capacity that by using their wealth for good, "they will lay up treasure for themselves as a firm foundation for the coming age, so that they may take hold of the life that is truly life" (1 Timothy 6:19).

It's not wrong to lay up treasure for yourself! But you do so not by hanging on to every last penny, but by seeking ways to "be rich in good deeds." Many Christians, especially the wealthy, tend to think that their financial gifts pay off any responsibility they have to use their human giftedness for the sake of others. But when I speak with groups of Christians who run or support foundations, I leave before them one reminder and one challenge.

Here's the reminder: When you spend half of your life giving away money, it's easy to forget that Jesus washed feet. True ministry is holistic, not just about finances.

And here's the challenge: just as the Master gave of Himself—not merely of His resources—so must we. That's what it means to be rich in good deeds.

23

AH, CONTENTMENT!

I fondly remember my days as a young college student at Azusa Pacific University. When I wasn't attending classes, I had a job working on the loading dock at the Robinson's warehouse in the City of Industry. I made a hundred dollars a week, tithed ten dollars, shared rent with four other guys, paid my tuition, drove a ten-year-old car, and still managed to meet all my expenses (just barely).

Yet my life felt full.

Though one could easily identify my unmet needs—my mom kept telling me I needed to buy new clothes—I felt content. I knew my life had a purpose. I was there to serve God, first by finishing school so that I could get into seminary, and second through my work.

During my time at Robinson's, I managed to become friends with every worker on the dock. For most Christians, such an achievement might seem quite difficult; dock workers tend to be hard-living, hard-cussing men who joyfully tell you church is for sissies. But their lifestyles never shocked me, since I had been reared by a former marine. I just took it all in stride. When I didn't faint from horror at their behavior and managed to maintain who and what I was despite their antics, they began to accept me. Before long, they considered me one of the guys and even began approaching me with their own issues and struggles.

Yes, I learned early on to be content with little!

But could I learn to be content with much?

A Difficult Task

The apostle Paul managed to accomplish something that very often escapes us: he felt content in both want and abundance. He wrote:

> I have learned to be content whatever the circum-stances. I know what it is to be in need, and I know what it is to have plenty. I have learned the secret of being content in any and every situation, whether well fed or hungry, whether living in plenty or in want. (Philippians 4:11–12)

For many of us, it would take a miracle to master content-ment in any one sphere of reality. But of the two states the apostle mentions, maybe it's easier for us to master contentment in a state of want.

Think back to the time just after you got married, or when you attended college, or as you began a new ministry. Remem-ber when the resources were slim and the lifestyles Spartan? Most of the Christians of capacity I know tell me they have very fond memories of those times. Many even secretly wish they could recapture those days (especially the married couples).

> *Contentment and ambition are not opposites.*
> *In fact, they can joyfully coexist.*

Why is that? I think it's because life in those beginning stages was filled with purpose. We were occupied with some specific, worthy task and filled with a vision of where we wanted to go. We weren't "there" yet and we hadn't lived long enough for the difficulties of life to beat our dreams out of us. And so we felt content.

But if my purpose in serving God during times of want was more than enough to keep me content, then why doesn't a sense of divine purpose keep me content during times of great abundance? Some people point to ambition as the culprit.

Ambition vs. Contentment

Is ambition the opposite of contentment? Some folks quote 1 Timothy 6:6, where Paul writes, "Godliness with contentment is great gain," and they say, "You just have to cease striving."

But if that were true, then it's hard to understand why Paul would also say things like this:

> It has always been my *ambition* to preach the Gospel where Christ was not known, so that I would not be building on someone else's foundation (Romans 15:20).

Make it your *ambition* to lead a quiet life, to mind your own business and to work with your hands, just as we told you, so that your daily life may win the respect of outsiders and so that you will not be dependent on anybody (1 Thessalonians 4:11–12).

Therefore we also have as our *ambition*, whether at home or absent, to be pleasing to Him (2 Corinthians 5:9, NASB).

Contentment and ambition are not opposites.

In fact, they can joyfully coexist.

Contentment means to be at peace with a situation, to have no anxiety over it. That's why Paul could have an *ambition* to preach the Gospel to unreached peoples while still having *peace* that God had him at just the right spot, wherever he found himself.

But if ambition doesn't keep us from contentment, then what does?

Contentment and Wealth

How many of us live anxious lives, worrying that we haven't done enough or given enough to satisfy the Lord? That always has been part of my struggle, and even today it sometimes rears its troubling head, making me wonder if I have done all that I could.

A lot of preaching reinforces this notion, because (I suspect) pastors fear that unless they stoke the fires, we will all become lounge lizards, resting in the grace of God rather than being motivated by the call of God. In the meanwhile, we struggle with how to live free of anxiety without becoming purposeless with our time, talents, and treasures. How can we know when we have satisfied God's design for our lives and wealth?

I believe we may find some help by evaluating how we have stewarded our wealth to this point. Do we have a greater sense of clarity and purpose today on how to use it in God-honoring ways than we did in the past? If not, I see two possibilities.

First, we may have lost our intentionality in discovering how God wants us to use what He has entrusted to us. All too often I hear that giving 10 percent of our wealth to God is a finish line, when in reality it is merely a starting point.

Second, if you are continually striving to learn how God wants to use you, without much success, it is very possible that He has you in a season of rest. Don't forget that God has created a "rhythm to life" that involves both work and rest. If you want to build muscle in your body, for example, you need both work and rest. The stress of the workout breaks down the muscle, while the rest period restores and grows it. In a similar way, God strategically uses periods of rest in our lives to prepare us for more effective service. Abraham, Moses, Paul, and even Jesus Himself all had quiet periods of preparation before launching into their ministries.

When Paul counseled a group of new Christians in Corinth, he gave them some very significant advice: "Don't be wishing you were someplace else or with someone else. Where you are right now is God's place for you. Live and obey and love and believe right there. God, not your [station in life], defines your life" (1 Corinthians 7:17, MSG).

Instead of striving to be more useful to God, strive to be content where God has placed you at this moment in time. You may not feel you belong there, but it helps neither you nor anyone else to spend your life and resources in totally aimless ways. The phrase "Ready, fire, aim" describes all too well much of the church today. We waste a ton of resources because we lack the patience to wait on God to reveal His path for us. So strive to be content in your relationship with God *where you are*, and then pray and cautiously probe and explore for where He may want you.

Wait upon God to reveal to you His purpose. And until He does, rest in Him and be content.

Remember, too, that the only effortless way to achieve contentment with your wealth is to not care or to remain indifferent to God's desire and will. While anxiety is the opposite of contentment, not caring how wealth can negatively impact your family for generations comes pretty close.

Fred Smith, president of the Gathering, wrote in one of his weekly e-mails to the Gathering family:

> Contentment is not the elimination of desire, nor is it the never-ending attempt to quash your ambition or convince yourself you have enough. It is not measuring your life by how much you subtract. This always leads to a life of discontent. Real contentment comes first from believing that God has good work for you to do—and then knowing that God has given you what you need to accomplish this work. It focuses less on having the "right amount" and more on accomplishing (and enjoying) the purpose He has set out for you.

Believe in the Sent One

Until we can feel valuable to God for who we are, we will never be able to discover the purpose God has for us, or the contentment that Paul describes. Jesus reminded us of this fact when He answered the question, "What must we do to do the works that God requires?" The Lord replied simply, "The work of God is this: to believe in the one He has sent" (John 6:29).

Who we are is rooted *solely* in our relationship to Christ. When that becomes our reality, then we will find the contentment that Paul promises can be ours.

24

CHECK YOUR MOTIVES

During our first years of getting the Sacred Harvest Foundation going, I began to hear some great testimonies about how others had given a significant portion of their money to kingdom work. The stories thrilled me, giving me a glimpse of exciting new horizons.

But to some extent, at least, I still remained in the shadow of the rich young ruler paradigm—a fact that tempered my joy.

Although I no longer feared we had failed to do enough, I now started thinking that I had to lead by example in extraordinary ways. I thought I had to demonstrate generosity and sacrifice on an unusual scale. I longed to demonstrate a kind of largeness of giving that would arrest the attention of others and inspire them to do more for God than they ever imagined.

If that sounds noble, it's only because I haven't mentioned a big underlying motive. One huge impulse that drove me had nothing to do with obedience.

In fact, I think I just wanted to outdo others.

Bigger Footprints

When I heard testimony after testimony of faithful Christians who had used great chunks of their wealth to serve others, I did think, *Wow, that's inspiring!* I did want to emulate their faithfulness… up to a point. Really, though, I didn't want to follow in their footsteps so much as make bigger footprints, out farther ahead.

I wanted to make a difference for Christ. I wanted to set an example for others and become a role model for them, but really, I wanted to be the best example and a leading role model. Somehow, one bit of advice from the apostle Paul had completely slipped my mind. I forgot that he had written:

> Each one should test his own actions. Then he can take pride in himself, *without comparing himself to somebody else*, for each one should carry his own load. (Galatians 6:4–5, emphasis added)

My load was trying to figure out how to manage the much-larger-than-I-ever-thought-they'd-be resources we had started to receive. My first instinct, as I've explained, was simply to give it away—then I wouldn't have to bother with the question anymore and I could go on thinking as I'd always thought, that poverty was next to godliness.

When it became clear that such a plan was not God's plan, I started looking for other ways to rid myself of the dilemma. While it might not please God for us to divest ourselves of the estate merely to make my problem go away, perhaps it would serve His purposes if we gave it away so that we could become shining examples for others to follow?

> *I know that recognition feels good. Recognition feeds us. But if we let that legitimate feeling get out of hand, it can lead to trouble.*

I quickly ran into two main problems with that line of thinking. One I've already mentioned: the estate was not mine to give away. It belonged to Susie and that hadn't changed, nor would it. And second, I didn't want merely to become an example to others; I wanted to become the *best* example, the *principal* example, the *chief* example. I wanted not only to take pride in myself, as Paul had said, but contrary to his counsel, I wanted to do so *by comparing myself with everyone else*.

While comparisons can provide some help in certain contexts (see, for example, 2 Corinthians 8:8), much of the time we want to compare ourselves with others simply so we can feel better about ourselves. We want to justify our actions or lifestyles, and comparisons can help us achieve a certain kind of emotional strength: "I'm doing better than Mr. Smith and Mrs. Jones, so I'm okay."

Unfortunately, however, Theodore Roosevelt had it right. Comparison really is the thief of joy. Comparison often leads to both jealousy and selfish ambition, both of which threatened my own spiritual life, and so James reminded me, "Where jealousy and selfish ambition exist, there will be disorder and every vile practice" (James 3:16). While I wanted to become a role model, I certainly did *not* want to be an example of "disorder and every vile practice"!

The writer of Proverbs had accurately diagnosed my condition millennia before my birth. He had written, "A tranquil heart gives life to the flesh, but envy makes the bones rot" (Proverbs 14:30).

Rotten bones. It's not the most flattering of biblical pictures. What's appealing about a decaying skeletal structure? But that's the analogy God's Spirit chose to illustrate a subtle danger to God's people.

Envy makes the bones rot very often through the cancer of unwise comparison. You want to be a terrific role model? Great! You want to be a more acclaimed role model than Billy or Jimmy? Not so great. (Smells kind of rotten.)

I wanted to give away our wealth, at least in part, so that I could win the approval of the people I most admired. But in doing so, I had forgotten another insight from Paul's Galatian letter. "Am I saying this now to win the approval of people or God?" he asked them. "Am I trying to please people? If I were still trying to please people, I would not be Christ's servant" (Galatians 1:10). I might not fully have understood my motivation at the time, but by trying to figure out how to convince Susie to sell her share in the family business, I wanted desperately to try to please and impress people, every bit as much as I wanted to please and honor Christ. One way we tried to avoid that entanglement was to give anonymously.

I'm glad to say that I no longer struggle as much with unwise comparison as I once did. These days, Susie and I do a certain amount of our giving anonymously. But while that makes sense in many cases, anonymous giving has its own problems.

Anonymity in Giving

Our internal motivations often have a way of cloaking themselves. Because each of us naturally wants to think of ourselves in positive terms, we have a normal tendency to reframe negative aspects as good, or provide rationales that explain why something that looks shabby is actually noble, or throw up a lot of dust to make it difficult to see the issue in a clear light.

You have to know yourself well. If you think you want to give some gift out of pride, then keep it quiet. Susie and I haven't put our names on various projects we've helped launch because we didn't want the notoriety. Still, I know that recognition feels good. Recognition feeds us. But if we let that legitimate feeling get out of hand, it can lead to trouble.

In a 2002 episode of *The King of Queens* called "Patrons Ain't," the sitcom's two main characters, Doug and Carrie Heffernan, start feeling guilty about their lack of charitable contributions to worthy causes. When they learn about a fund-raiser for a local elementary school library, they make a hefty donation. They expect to get their names on a bronze plaque that lists large donors. But when they show up for a celebration at the library, they can't find their names on the memorial. That unwelcome discovery leads to a ton of laughs as the couple, and especially Carrie, seeks to get the recognition they said they didn't need.

It's easy for a donor's motivations to go a little sideways. More than once I've heard someone say, "I wanted to get on somebody's radar, so I sent a large gift to his ministry." It usually works.

Sir John Templeton thought anonymity in giving was required at two times:

1. When pride or ego drive one's giving.
2. When one's giving might cause the recipient great embarrassment.

My question is, when you give anonymously, how do you set your light upon a hill? When you give anonymously, how do you give glory to God so that others may see your good works and praise your Father in heaven? Anonymous giving can sometimes be like putting your light under a basket.

Many years ago, our daughter gave an anonymous $700 scholarship to enable a beloved teacher to go on a school mission trip. She used her own money and made the decision completely on her own. She asked me to take the gift to the school but not let anyone know who had made the donation.

The school's principal accepted the gift with gratitude, but later returned to say, "The teacher was very thankful but troubled by not knowing who to thank for the gift." My daughter's anonymous gift had the unintended consequence of preventing the recipient from completing her joy by being able to say, "Thank you!" to her.

Yes, there is a time for anonymous giving. But there's also a time to let your light shine.

Skip the Fast Track

Jack Canfield, author of the *Chicken Soup for the Soul* series, once said, "I generally find that comparison is the fast track to unhappiness. No one ever compares themselves to someone else and comes out even. Nine times out of ten, we compare ourselves to people who are somehow better than us and end up feeling more inadequate."

Don't go down that road. Skip that particular fast track. Forget about comparing yourself with others and strive simply to do what you believe God is calling *you* to do. That's the road to happiness and fulfillment—and a thousand other treasures God has waiting for you.

25

A VESSEL FOR NOBLE PURPOSES

M aybe you've met some Christians who loathe the very idea of Christmas trees.

I've met a few; you might call them evangelists on the subject. They get really worked up. They will tell you (without much encouragement) that the tradition of yuletide trees is deeply pagan and has no place in a true believer's life. They will inform you, with a great gusto, that the ancient Romans celebrated the winter solstice in a feast called Saturnalia, held in honor of Saturnus, the god of agriculture. The old pagans decorated their homes with green foliage and lights and exchanged gifts of coins, pastries, and lamps.

They also will tell you that ancient priests called Druids used evergreens to celebrate their own shadowy winter solstice rituals in Great Britain many centuries ago. These pagans used holly and mistletoe to symbolize eternal life and affixed evergreen branches over doorways to ward off evil spirits.

"I don't see how any 'Christian' can have a Christmas tree," they will say. "It's a pagan celebration, not a Christian one! You might as well set up an idol in your house."

While I suppose this is one of those issues about which the

apostle Paul might say, "Each one should be fully convinced in his own mind" (Romans 14:5), my own convictions lie elsewhere. An old tradition says that one Christmas Eve Martin Luther took a walk through some snowy woods and there saw some evergreen trees laden with snow and glistening in the moonlight. Their beauty so inspired him that after he returned home, he cut down a fir tree, set it up in his house, and decorated it with candles. He told his children about his glorious experience and then lit the tree's candles to help his family remember and honor the birth of the Christ child.

Since the very beginning, the church has always taken that which is ignoble, outside of God's realm and kingdom, and baptized it to make it noble. That's what Luther did with the Christmas tree, which for millions of Christians worldwide now symbolizes God's redemption through Christ.

Set Apart for God's Holy Purposes

Luther didn't initiate this pattern of taking ignoble things and making them noble. The apostle Paul got the ball rolling very early in Christian history through his second letter to his young protégé, Timothy:

> In a large house there are articles not only of gold and silver, but also of wood and clay; some are for noble purposes and some for ignoble. If a man cleanses himself from the latter, he will be an instrument for noble purposes, made holy, useful to the Master and prepared to do any good work. (2 Timothy 2:20–21).

When Paul uses the terms *noble* and *ignoble*, he's tapping into a common scene that members of every Jewish household would recognize. To this day, many Jewish homes have a complete set of Passover dishes, used only for the Passover; those are the "noble" articles. The remaining dishes in the home are intended for ordinary, everyday use; they are "ignoble," not set apart for some special divine purpose.

The word translated as *holy*, like the word *sacred*, means "set apart" or "separated for some special purpose." It refers to something specially designated and singled out for God's specific use. Paul uses this metaphor to tell us something important, not about dishes, but about ourselves.

The ignoble things in our lives are those items we claim as our own. "Mine!" we say of them. They serve no purpose other than what we establish. For many of us, our wealth once fit into this category, sometimes for decades.

> *Vision, in and of itself, is never sufficient to bring about a new future. In fact, vision doesn't even sell much anymore. It's the ability to deliver on that vision that sells.*

But even ignoble things can be made noble, holy, when we choose to set them apart for God's purposes. Paul says a man can "cleanse himself," or set himself apart for noble purposes, even if for years he was like an "unclean" dish, suitable only for ignoble purposes. When an individual lays down his ignoble past for a noble present and future, he becomes "useful to the Master and prepared to do any good work." Both he and his possessions live under God's rule from then on and remain constantly available for God to use according to His plan and purpose.

More Than a Vision

The switch from ignoble to noble involves more than possessions, of course. It also includes how we use our talents, abilities, connections, influence, and everything else. That means it also affects our leadership.

Back in the '90s, it seemed that everyone was trying to "sell a vision." A lot of those visions went bust. Vision, in and of itself, is never sufficient to bring about a new future. In fact, vision doesn't even sell much anymore. It's the ability to *deliver* on that vision that sells. A good vision is critical, of course, but if you have no proven track record that you can produce what you envision, it's a hard push.

A leading foundation consultant makes the suggestion that, as funders, we don't go to a ministry to tell them what the great idea is; they have to *know* what the great idea is. And we don't go in to tell them what the need is; they have to *know* what the need is. Our job is to provide the capacity they need in order to mobilize the idea to meet the need.

I would throw a fourth factor into the mix. You not only need a great idea to meet a great need, and great capacity to fund the idea, but all of this requires great leadership. Mark this well: without appropriate leadership, the venture—*any* venture—will flounder and fail. For many of us, part of exchanging an ignoble past for a noble present may involve a willingness to provide strong leadership for worthy initiatives that currently lack it.

Our work as a foundation takes all four factors into consideration. We provide the capacity and believe in a ministry's vision, but if a group is not meeting what we consider a critical need or doesn't have the leadership necessary to deliver on its vision, then we seldom even bother with it. How many good ideas fail because they lack good leadership? I don't know, but it's a lot. What would happen if successful Christian businesspeople decided to take their "ignoble" experience and make it "noble" so that God could use it in some good work for His kingdom? It almost boggles the mind.

And by the way, real leadership doesn't mean "taking over," either. Author Henry Blackaby says the thing that really disturbs him about many new pastors today is that they march into a congregation and act as though the Holy Spirit has never been active in that body before. Such leaders therefore do not recognize the unique giftedness in the church or that God already may have an intended purpose for that body. Instead, they plow in like a first-term president of the United States, bringing in their outside agenda and totally ignoring everything God already has done in that congregation. They also frequently dismiss whatever God has gifted that body to do.

Effective leaders, by contrast, go into such a situation asking, "What has God been doing in this place already? And how can I partner with it?" They know they can't just come in and impose something radically new. It will never work. They figure out how to get fresh ideas bubbling up from below and get other ideas dribbling down from above and then look for a place in the middle where the two meet. That's the core they build around.

If leadership is influence, then where does that influence come from? It comes from trust; trust generates influence. When people trust you, they become far more open to being influenced by you. And what is trust built upon? Genuine relationships. People don't trust what they don't know.

But when a leader is a known commodity, a "vessel for noble purposes" who has established good relationships and created good outcomes in the past, trust and influence naturally follow.

Be Patient

The switch from ignoble to noble doesn't necessarily happen all at once, or even very quickly. Sometimes, the metamorphosis from one to the other takes a while.

Consider once again the American Christmas tree tradition. Most historians think it probably came to this country on the backs of Hessian troops during the American Revolution, or perhaps with German immigrants to Pennsylvania and Ohio. But however it came, it didn't spread like wildfire.

In New England, the Puritans banned the celebration of Christmas, which obviously included a prohibition against Christmas trees. A Cleveland minister almost lost his job in 1851 because he allowed someone to put up a tree in his church. Students in Boston were expected to be in class on Christmas

Day as late as 1870, and some schools even expelled students who chose instead to stay home with their families and Christmas trees.

So if you still struggle with a personal transition from ignoble to noble, don't sweat it too much. Sing a verse from "O Tannenbaum" and let Martin Luther's snowy evening in the woods give you encouragement to keep on going.

26

HUNTERS AND NESTERS

Y es, as a matter of fact, opposites *do* attract.

My experience as a pastor has taught me that in most marriages you will often find that one spouse has a more visionary and risk-taking bent, while the other tends to be more conservative and cautious.

Sociologists refer to this phenomenon as "hunters and nesters." Hunters feel most comfortable with living life one day at a time, focusing on new challenges, and taking promising risks. Rather than saving for a rainy day, they will risk it all for a dream, yes, even God's dream. Nesters, on the other hand, like to build nests. They feel most secure when they have everything close at hand, knowing not only where tomorrow's resources are coming from but also where they'll get next month's allowances.

Susie and I are typical specimens. Our biggest conflicts about money did not erupt over how to spend it, but how to give it away. I loved the challenge of giving and spoke of many noble visions for God's work, while Susie lived with the mind-set that by tomorrow we might be broke. In our household, I was the liberal spender but also the liberal giver. Susie was the conservative spender and a conservative giver.

When I tried to live by faith, Susie was more comfortable in living by sight. She needed to *see* what was in our bank account. It took me sixteen years of marriage to figure out that if I could show Susie a big enough nest, she would feel secure enough to expand her faith in giving.

The Contours of the Conflict

Our struggle dates all the way back to our time in the pastorate. When Susie and I would give our tithes and offerings, I would track it like a Pharisee. I wouldn't give to the penny, but I'd round up, ballparking it high rather than low.

So as soon as Susie would receive her quarterly distributions, I got ready to start writing out the checks to our favorite charities. She inevitably would ask, "Can't I at least hold it in my hand for a while?"

"If we don't do it now, we're going to forget," I'd reply.

But I would usually wait, making sure to mentally track all we needed to give. I'd come back a month or two later and say, "Susie, we still have all this money we need to give."

"But we already gave a bunch of money," she often responded.

For Susie, spreading out our tithes throughout the year made her feel as if we were always giving, giving, and giving. She had a hard time remembering that at the same time, we were also receiving, receiving, receiving as well as saving, saving, saving. A smart financial adviser will tell clients to have six months' salary and expenses in savings. We did that and more, but since Susie never saw it (or lacked immediate access to it), it always felt to her as though we were continually on the verge of running out of savings.

> *It took me sixteen years of marriage to figure out that if I could show Susie a big enough nest, she would feel secure enough to expand her faith in giving.*

That meant that every time we received a distribution, we'd have a disagreement. Should we or shouldn't we give a portion of it? I always won by imposing scriptural guilt.

My beloved wife has little concept of the amount of money she actually has, which is both good and bad. For her, the difference between a million dollars and ten thousand dollars is just a couple of zeros. She has this sense that, "Tomorrow, we could be broke." Could we *really* lose everything tomorrow, other than what we have in the bank (which could last for a couple of years)? Sure.

"But if that's the case," I said, "Jesus is coming. And if you know you're going up there, then don't worry about it."

The whole situation became an unceasing tug-of-war for us.

At first, I chalked up the difficulty to her focus, her habit of looking at how much we gave rather than how much we received.

To me, our situation felt like the man who tithed all his life.

When he made fifty dollars a week, he gave five dollars. When he made one hundred dollars, he gave ten. At five hundred a week, he gave fifty, and when he reached one thousand, he gave one hundred. No problem. But when he started making five thousand dollars a week, he thought, *Man, five hundred is a lot of money to be giving away every week.* So he went to his pastor.

"Pastor" he said, "I've been a tither all my life, but five hundred dollars a week is a lot of money to give."

His pastor looked him in the eye and replied, "Do you want to remain a tither?"

"Yes," the man answered.

"Then let's pray," said the pastor. "Dear Lord, our brother here has always been a tither, but he thinks five hundred dollars a week is too much. So to help him to feel comfortable with his tithe once more, please reduce his income."

That's how Susie sounded to me. It took me years to finally figure out that Susie wasn't focusing on how much we gave, but on her need as a nester for security. She was like the ants praised in Proverbs 6:6, "who store up their food in the summer." I was trying to do the same thing, but in a different way. Investing our money by putting the funds out of sight, out of mind, meant that I felt no temptation to spend it. But the strategy worked against Susie, because she could not see, touch, or access her nest, and thus received no sense of security. If we were to grow in our generosity and minimize the debates, I knew we needed to change how we operated.

I figured we needed to do two things, right away.

First, we opened a charity checking account. Every time Susie received a dividend, our tithes and offerings went into it. That way, whenever we gave a gift, it came from the charity account rather than our savings. This helped Susie to see that we were not taking money from our savings. It also minimized her concern that we put a constant drain on our funds whenever we withdrew an amount to make a gift.

Years later, we discovered a more tax-efficient "charity checkbook" called a giving fund at the National Christian Foundation. When we put our tithes and offerings into our giving fund, we get a tax write-off at the time of deposit. So rather than feel hurried at the end of each year to give our tithes in order to reap the benefit of a tax write-off, we can store our tithes in our giving fund. This enables us to take more time to diligently investigate where and when we give to a ministry. NCF gave us a way to establish a family foundation so we didn't have to incur the great expense of setting up a private foundation that mandates that one file tax returns each year, while giving information that becomes part of the public record.

Second, we did something to take the tension out of our giving. Rather than stash our surplus monies in less liquid, more interest-bearing assets, we let Susie's checking account build up to about six months of expenses. By keeping this larger-than-average checking account—admittedly not a very wise investment strategy—we found a better investment strategy for us to give to God's kingdom. This arrangement gave Susie the security she needed, for she could see every day what she had in her account and that she didn't need to worry about our ability to meet our obligations. She now had a beautiful surplus, which greatly relaxed her. She could see it. She could touch it. She knew we had committed a specified amount of money to kingdom causes, so no problem.

Best of all for us as a couple, these two simple moves

tremendously minimized our debates. We still have good discussions about where and how much to give, but our continual haggling over it has become a thing of the past.

A Wonderful Surprise

The result of our two-pronged plan surprised even me. Formerly when Susie received her quarterly disbursements, she would ask me how much we needed to put in our charity account. After the new plan went into effect, she didn't do that anymore.

One Sunday after church, she casually informed me that she had put our tithe in the charity account. I immediately asked how much she had put in, because I wanted to make sure she remembered that we had agreed upon increasing our percentage of giving. When she told me the amount she deposited, my jaw dropped. She had put in *10 percent more* than our prior level of giving, all on her own initiative.

I don't know if I have ever felt more proud of my wife.

And I don't think she ever felt more joy.

27

CAN HE USE WHAT HE
ALREADY OWNS?

S ince my high school days, I've always had a thing for cars.
I used to own a '65 Mustang convertible that I bought from
my father-in-law. It needed a little restoration, just a quick paint
job, and then I'd enjoy driving it.

But that simple paint job soon ballooned into a whole lot
more. First, I carefully painted the car a beautiful Porsche
Guards red. Then I redid the interior with a red-and-white
pony interior to match. But then, so that the engine bay would
match the quality of the interior and exterior, I also had to give
that a new paint job—and then have it detailed to look like new.

Before long, I was the proud owner of a show-quality
Mustang. Its first time out, it took first place in its division!
How happy do you think I felt as the owner? At the outset, it
felt *great*.

In a very short time, however, my joy turned to misery.
After I had put so much time and effort and money into that car,
something unexpected happened: I became afraid to drive it.

I couldn't go to the store for fear that somebody might ding
the door.

I wouldn't take it on trips for fear that someone would steal it.

I didn't dare to use it to do quick, simple errands for fear that its paint might get scratched, or a flying rock would crack its windshield, or I'd spill something on the seats.

In two years, I sold the thing. Why? Because I had lost the use of my car.

The real joy of anything, no matter what, whether big or small, never really comes from ownership, but in its use. Ownership apart from use has no value.

God's Greater Concern

All too often we make the mistake of thinking that *God's* primary concern is ownership. We think that, more than anything, He wants us to recognize that He owns everything we have.

Well, *of course* He owns it all. So He says to a chastened Job, "Who has a claim against me that I must pay? Everything under heaven belongs to me" (Job 41:11). The irony here is that it makes no difference whether we acknowledge His ownership or not; He already *does* own it all, regardless of what we may think.

I think God's far greater concern, much more than whether we recognize His universal ownership, is this: *Do we give Him the use of our wealth?* I first heard that idea from Ray Lyne, who insisted usage is always more valuable than ownership.

While God owns everything He makes, sometimes He lacks the ability to use the things He has entrusted to us. He would like to use them for His glory and wise purposes, but like confused stewards, we say, "No, I don't think so. This is *mine*. I may let you use that over there, but this precious thing belongs to me. Hands off!"

> *We must always hold whatever we have in our hands ever so loosely, so that when the Lord comes and says to us, "I have need of it," we are willing and eager to respond.*

I believe we all have things in our lives that we do not recognize as gifts from God. Maybe we refuse to open our hands to Him out of fear that if we give this special thing to God, He may take it away from us for good. Or maybe we never offer Him the use of something He's given us because it never occurred to us that the thing we have is the very thing God might actually like to use.

How much wiser it would be, and how much happier we would be, if we gladly surrendered to Him whatever He's already given to us, so that it remains available for Him to use as He pleases! This doesn't mean He uses it 24/7. I doubt that happens very often, in fact. It really means that at certain times and for specific reasons, God may have need of it for this or that opportunity. And when He's done with it, more than likely He'll return it to you so that you can continue to use it in your day-to-day course of living.

Scripture has a great word picture that clearly illustrates

for me what it means to live with our wealth in a God-pleasing way. The story I have in mind comes from Palm Sunday.

As Jesus and His disciples approached Jerusalem toward the end of His earthly ministry, He sent two apostles into a village to accomplish a fairly unusual task. Jesus told them that just as they entered the village, they would find "a colt tied there, which no one has ever ridden. Untie it and bring it here."

I can picture the two disciples standing there, looking nervously at one another and thinking, *Uh, but what if someone sees us? Won't they think we're thieves?*

Without waiting for them to ask the question, Jesus quickly answered it. He instructed them, "If anyone asks you, 'Why are you doing this?' tell him, 'The Lord needs it and will send it back here shortly'" (Mark 11:2–3).

The two disciples did just as they were told, and sure enough, some people standing near the animal said to them, "What are you doing, untying that colt?" The pair of nervous disciples recited the answer Jesus had given them and the onlookers immediately let them go. When the men brought the colt to Jesus, He sat on it and rode it into Jerusalem in what has become known as "the triumphal entry." On that memorable first Palm Sunday, Jesus announced himself as the rightful king of Israel, the long-awaited Messiah of God's chosen people. It was quite a majestic scene!

But have you ever wondered what happened to the colt after Jesus finished with it? The text strongly implies that Jesus immediately had it returned to its owner. And what do you suppose the owner did with it? Did he kill it, stuff it, and place it over his mantle with a sign attached: "Jesus rode here"? Of course not. The colt got returned to its owner so that it could resume the purpose it had before Jesus requested its use—carrying firewood or water, perhaps, or helping the owner with his trade.

It is no different with us. God gives us many things so that we might provide for our families, use them in our business, or even just to enjoy them. The story of the colt instructs us that, as stewards, we must always hold whatever we have in our hands ever so loosely, so that when the Lord comes and says to us, "I have need of it," we are willing and eager to respond. Many times, perhaps most of the time, God will return to us what He has chosen to use until He has need of it again.

The same principle appears in the parable of the shrewd steward that we considered in chapter eleven. At the end of that story, Jesus told His listeners, "I tell you, use worldly wealth to gain friends for yourselves, so that when it is gone, you will be welcomed into eternal dwellings" (Luke 16:9).

The operative term there is the word *use*.

Use worldly wealth, Jesus said.

He didn't say, "give away" or "reject" or "donate" or "lose." He didn't say, "downplay your worldly wealth" or "feel ashamed of your worldly wealth." No, He instructed His followers to *use* worldly wealth in order to achieve some worthy purpose.

When we offer to God our resources for His use—resources that belong to Him already—in a way, we're redeeming those things for a higher purpose. We're saying, "This is Yours—please use it however You see fit."

A book titled *Biblical Financial Study* from Crown Financial Ministries includes a quitclaim deed that students can use to "sign over to God" their possessions. The middle of the form says, "I (we) hereby transfer to the Lord the ownership of the following possessions," and then includes a chunk of white space in which students can list various possessions. Two small columns at the bottom of the form complete the deed. The one on the left features the words, "Witnesses who will hold me (us) accountable in the recognition of the Lord's ownership," followed by four blank lines, while the one on the right says simply, "Stewards of the possessions above," with two signature lines below.

I found this all quite interesting. And then the question hit me: What do *you* need to sign over to God?

Make God Excited

Ownership is not God's biggest concern. It is all His, whether we acknowledge it or not. When we leave the world, it all gets left behind. We take nothing, not any of us.

What God really yearns for is to have use of the wealth—time, talent, treasure—that He has entrusted to us. When He finally gets to use what He's given to us, I think He gets excited. He says, "You mean I get to play with what I gave you? Let's do something great together!"

Those who steward their wealth to benefit its rightful owner experience two realities. First, they get entrusted with more. And second, they receive an invitation to enter into their master's happiness (see Matthew 25:14–23). When we live with God's blessings in accordance with His purposes, we will receive not only further blessings, but we will walk the path to contentment, the joy of the Lord.

28

HONOR THE LORD
WITH YOUR WEALTH

A t every chapel I attended during my time at my Lutheran
Bible school, we took an offering. Afterward, we always
celebrated by clapping. We wanted to express what a great
privilege and honor it was to give back to God what He had
first given to us.

Giving is never to be a transaction between man and God.
We don't give in order to get. We give because we already have
been given to. Giving is an act of thanksgiving for the blessings and grace that God has bestowed upon us. It is how we
honor and worship God for His unmerited favor and blessings.
"Honor the LORD with your wealth, with the first fruits of all
your crops," says Proverbs 3:9.

Living Under God's Lordship

Stewarding what God has entrusted to us is not a multiple-
choice question. Just as God seeks to redeem the whole world
so that all of creation may live under His lordship, so He desires

that everything that we are and everything we have should also live under His lordship.

Jesus declared that He did not come into the world to abolish the law, but to fulfill it. A curious thing happened as a result: Jesus *expanded* the meaning of God's law. Killing now includes anger; adultery is an emotional affair as much as it is a physical one.

Giving is no different. When Jesus and New Testament writers speak of giving, they never use the word *tithe* to describe how one should give.* Instead, they expand the standard to include a God-honoring gift—generous, joyful, and without compulsion. By contrast, while the Pharisees tithed from everything they owned, Jesus *never* praised their gifts.

Wise Giving Today

We honor the Lord most in our giving when we give wisely. And wise giving tends to take time, effort, and planning. That means that a lot of last-minute giving, almost by definition, *isn't* wise.

Did you know that the majority of ministries/nonprofits report that 30 to 50 percent of their annual budget comes in during the last two months of the year? This means that most of us do the majority of our giving at the end of the year. Why?

There are good reasons and not so good reasons.

---

* The word *tenth* is used to describe Old Testament giving in Matthew 23:23, Luke 11:42 and 18:12, and several times in Hebrews 7 in reference to Abraham's giving to the mysterious figure Melchizedek.

> *Wise giving tends to take time, effort, and planning. That means that a lot of last-minute giving, almost by definition, isn't wise.*

For some of us, a sizable portion of our income depends upon bonuses or distributions, often made at the end of the year. It is difficult to plan your charitable giving when you're uncertain of income.

But for others of us, end-of-the-year giving results from not being intentional about how we steward our resources for kingdom impact. We have given little thought as to how and where we will invest in God's kingdom. We have budgeted for vacations, household expenditures, schooling, taxes, etc., but have given little thought as to what we want to accomplish in Jesus's name. Consequently, we don't remember until the end of the year that we need to give if we want to take advantage of charitable gift tax savings. The result:

1. We end up giving from our "leftover" income for the year.
2. We give without much thought as to why we give.
3. Our decisions about where to give often depend upon Christmas mailings or some ministry we just heard about; we have no real understanding of who they are or what they do.

For Christians of capacity, who can easily give four- and five-figure gifts, it will prove beneficial—and wise—for the donor to have more information about the effectiveness and

efficiency of the ministry/nonprofit. It also makes sense to acquire some intimate knowledge of the organization so we can
direct our gifts in a way that enhances the ministry. We want
good ministries to flourish in their core calling and not allow
our gifts to divert them from their primary mission. This kind
of wise giving honors the Lord and maximizes the impact of
our gifts.

Our Own Giving Journey

Although these days Susie and I utilize about 15 percent of our
income to support our lifestyle, we both realize we are not living as simply as we could. Still, we give away anywhere from
two to three times what we spend on ourselves.

When Susie and I first set out to try to understand where
God wanted us to invest financially into His kingdom, we
started with a very broad net. We began with our home church.
Though churches may not always be the most exciting places in
the world in terms of innovation and mission, we realized that
even from the days of the Book of Acts, the church was always
God's primary means to bringing His *shalom* to the world. It
was also the primary place in which our family had been nur-
tured in the faith and our community was being served.

At the same time, we realized that we can do tremendous
harm to the church by making it dependent on us, a conundrum
that haunts many Christians of capacity. We want to support
our church, but how do we do so wisely, without creating a
sense of expectancy, entitlement, and dependence?

We purposely decided that our giving to the general fund

should never exceed more than 10 percent of its total (some suggest an even lower number). Another reason to limit such funding is the worst-case scenario: if the day ever comes when you can no longer give (death, relocation, etc.) the absence of your financial support will not paralyze a church's ability to continue serving. Yes, it may cause some serious adjustments, but it will not cause its demise.

When the time came for capital campaigns for construction or missions, sometimes we would provide matching gifts to help stimulate the congregation to take ownership of the work.

As we struggled with where to give outside of the church, we decided to explore an Acts 1:8 model: Jerusalem, Judea, Samaria, and the ends of the world. In more universal terms, we wanted to give locally, regionally, nationally, and internationally.

We also had to decide what *kind* of ministries we wanted to support, so we divided that into four parts as well: the church (building it up), compassion ministries (the Great Commandment), conversion ministries (the Great Commission), and our community. In time, we reduced this to three, as we believed that the Great Commandment and the Great Commission should never be divorced from one another, but rather should be treated as a seamless whole. We will not regularly support any ministry/nonprofit that focuses solely on either one of the two; both have to be present. Just as Jesus's ministry was both word and deed, so we look for those ministries that seek to be an enduring and endearing presence of Jesus in the lives of those they are called to serve, while always intentionally trying to bring individuals into a deep and profound relationship with Jesus.

After a couple of years of charting our giving, we noticed two discrepancies. First, the vast majority was going to the church segment, which meant very little was going to the compassion/conversion segment. Second, we noticed that we were extremely overweighted in funding US initiatives, which meant we had committed very little internationally.

While we didn't necessary want to treat all areas equally, we used this method to determine where our primary interests lay, as well as identify any blind spots.

And boy, did we find blind spots—especially internationally!

In years past, it wouldn't have bothered me much to find we were underserving the international world, as I, like many Christians, believe that the US has enough problems of its own. Not until I attended a Gathering Conference in San Diego in the late '90s did I realize how far off base we had drifted.

Keynote speaker Dr. John Stott offered a profound, biblically balanced view of giving. I came away reaffirmed that God gives each of us varying passions and interests for our giving, *but* (and here the arrow struck my heart) those passions and interests must never negate God's own passion and interests—and God has a tremendous interest in the world, not just in the US!

I once heard Sir John Templeton, noted for his international investing, explain his own rationale. He reminded people that European investors built America. Foreign money helped America begin to grow and flourish until our own money took over. He therefore considered it a responsibility for America to invest in other countries so that their economies also could prosper and create jobs.

Now go forward some fifteen years. While our international portfolio has grown to rival the one for the United States, we now find ourselves underfunding Orange County, the community in which we live and are called to serve. And so we have started to make some adjustments. When the target keeps moving, you must, as well.

Another Name for Discipleship

God calls us to steward all that we are and all that we have. But really, stewardship is nothing more than discipleship by another name.

We're stewards of the Gospel. We're trustees of the Gospel. We're keepers of the faith that God has imparted to us— and that includes everything that we own and everything that we are. When we steward our resources wisely, we honor God and become effective partners with Him in His ongoing kingdom work.

29

BE WISE

One of the best and choicest gifts God can give any of us is the gift of perspective.

It doesn't come bundled with a college degree.

It isn't stuck in the envelope along with a certificate of ordination.

You don't get it in your mailbox on a certain birthday.

You can't inherit it from your parents or even buy it online.

If God gives us a clear-eyed perspective on some aspect of life on this frequently confused planet, it's usually because He has guided us through a set of experiences—frequently painful—and allowed us to learn from them.

In His kindness, God has given me a unique viewpoint on wise giving as someone who is both a pastor, a major donor, and an individual who has served on many nonprofit boards.

Many churches and nonprofits consider a major donor someone who gives $5,000 to $10,000 or more a year to its support. Individuals who have the means to become major donors, but need to be developed or cultivated, may be classified as potential major donors. I consider the issue of the major donor to be very important for three reasons.

> *The chief guideline for major donors differs hardly*
> *at all from the Hippocratic Oath taken by doctors.*
> *Both groups must strive to do no harm.*

First, the unwise implementation of major donor gifts can injure the health of the organization and the ministry partner him/herself.

Second, major donors often are at best overlooked and at worse shunned in the church, except during major capital campaigns. Then they become everybody's friend.

Third, as the church becomes increasingly made up of new Christians who have no foundational understanding about stewardship, the major donor will become critical to the continued growth of an organization's ministry.

So how can Christians of capacity become *wise* major donors? I have a few suggestions.

Bane or Blessing

I have been counseled many times over the years that the chief guideline for major donors differs hardly at all from the Hippocratic Oath taken by doctors. Both groups must strive to do no harm.

How major donors relate both to the church and to other ministry organizations can create either bane or blessing. The bane manifests itself in four distinct ways. Some are quite obvious, while others are not.

1.   Dominance

Some major donors *want* their congregations/nonprofits to depend on them, for they see giving not as an act of worship, but as a means of exercising power, giving them control over ministry decisions and direction.

This phenomenon especially afflicts small churches that have been run by the same individuals or families for generations. Since pastoral stays in these churches tend to be very short, these donors never fully hand over the reins to the church. Why should they, they wonder, since the pastor will be gone in two or three years, anyway?

Other men and women in the congregation know this happens, but they allow the wealthy person to take control because they don't see a viable alternative. "Let him have his way" becomes the congregational motto.

On the other hand, the need for "ownership" or individual scrutiny of a ministry doesn't necessarily indicate a power play. People today rightly demand more ownership in the institutions where they invest their dollars, either requesting a voice as to where the money goes or asking for more personal involvement. Scrutiny also is rising in how the money gets managed. Where is it going? Who will lead this or that initiative? Christians of capacity didn't accumulate their wealth by blindly investing in businesses or ventures simply because someone in charge said it would be a good idea!

2. Dependence

I call this the Sugar Daddy Syndrome. It manifests itself in codependent language:

- "If so-and-so doesn't participate, we will never make it."
- "No need to worry, so-and-so will come through."
- "We can just sit back and let him pay for it all—he's got the money."

Again, this problem is probably more common in smaller churches or organizations that have some primary figure who provides a large portion of the budget. So what's the problem?

First, major donors can kill the people's divinely ordained stewardship mandate by letting them become dependent on the Sugar Daddy who pays the bills. *All* followers of Jesus need to give to support their church, so never do anything to compromise that.

Second, the Sugar Daddy Syndrome leads to a long-term liability. What if the donor does not renew his large pledge for the next year, and the church or organization made commitments based on this year's budget that will carry into the following year? Or what if the major donor leaves the organization for some reason?

For these reasons, it's probably best that no single donor give more than 10 percent of the organization's total operating budget. Others say less, but you be the judge. (Full disclosure: a few times our foundation has chosen to exceed the guideline of 10 percent to the operating budget. But we did so judiciously!) While wealthy donors can give more than 10 percent to specific causes, such as to special projects outside the operating budget, even then, no church or organization should let them fund the whole thing. Major donors can do the most good by becoming allies, perhaps by doing matching gifts, so that other supporters learn they must get involved if the whole enterprise is to thrive for the long term.

If you don't know whether your church or some favorite organization has become dependent upon you and your support, look for a very common, telltale sign. Whenever money gets tight in the organization, or it needs some big-ticket item, rather than dealing with issues of poor stewardship, does the pastor, board, or organizational representative run to you? That's the sign.

It may seem flattering to know that a church or organization depends on you, but after a while, you'll begin to realize that the dependency is becoming codependency. And no one likes being in those relationships.

3. Deference

When officials of an organization or members of a congregational leadership team begin to defer decision-making power to the major donor in order to get his or her support, it's time to quote Captain James Lovell of Apollo 13: "Houston, we've had a problem."

Do the leaders of the groups you support seem overly concerned about whether you feel offended by actions the organization has taken or plans to take? Do you get the impression that these leaders have come to believe you've "bought the right" to decide which direction the organization should go? If so, then deference has become a problem, both for the organization and for you.

One big clue that this has taken place shows up in what I call dancing for dollars. Pastors and heads of nonprofits feel a real temptation to go dancing for dollars, especially in capital campaigns, when majors donors get personally solicited to step up to the plate. Such appeals reveal a "We will do whatever is necessary to get their support" mind-set and usually go something like this: "We all know that Mr. Big Bucks will give $$$ to build the [fill in the blank] if we…"

- Go back to using the fifty-year-old hymnal (or return to some nostalgic practice).
- Move in this direction and do this program.
- Build a sixteenth-century pulpit, eight feet high (or revert to a cherished old slogan).
- Hire (or fire) this particular individual.

A variation of dancing for dollars is trolling for dollars, a questionable activity that particularly tempts entrepreneurial leaders. It occurs when such leaders visit a major donor or potential major donor to find out what interests them and then offer to do that thing if the donor will agree to fund it. Do you see the potential for disaster?

First, the new venture begins to spread the staff thin in order to satisfy the wishes of the donor, without paying any particular attention to the mission or goals of the organization.

Second, if the organization fails to meet the demands or expectations of the donor, it has wasted kingdom dollars and probably has lost the donor's support forever.

Third, such arrangements can create long-term commitments

that the organization will have to support in later years, lead-ing to cranky in-house conversations that sound a lot like this: "We never really wanted to do this, but that is what so-and-so demanded." That never leads to good morale, a healthy culture, or organizational success!

Getting deeply involved as a major donor in some campaign or process is not wrong, of course; all major campaigns seek to involve their major donors from the very beginning so that they gain a sense of ownership. It becomes wrong only if the process violates the integrity of the mission of the church or organization.

4. Indifference

We in the church have done much to alienate the wealthy in our communities. Why? I can think of several reasons:

- A desire to avoid looking as if we show partiality to the rich.
- A skewed piety that says money is evil and people who have money have screwed-up values.
- A flawed theology that insists people should never accumulate wealth, but rather give it all away.
- A new pastor comes into a church where the previous pastor was a crony to the rich, so the new leader de-cides to balance things out by ignoring the rich and becoming the one true friend of the middle class.
- A tendency to shun what we don't understand.
- A reaction of jealousy or feeling intimidated by people of wealth.

In an effort to show no favoritism to the rich and a desire to demonstrate they are not easily influenced by big money, some church leaders become indifferent, standoffish, or even condescending toward Christians of capacity. I know, because I came from *exactly* that kind of background.

Looking for Wise Stewards

We all want to become the kind of stewards God wants us to be, don't we? Yet that takes not only a caring heart, but wisdom. I like how one old preacher put it: "Wisdom and money can get you almost anything, but only wisdom can save your life" (Ecclesiastes 7:12, NLT).

Or the life of your church or favorite organization.

30

A WORD TO PASTORS

I have often said that the church tends to either use, abuse, or ignore the wealthy. Why does that happen?

Most of the time, I believe it's because pastors don't know what to do with rich people. The wealthy intimidate them; they can't relate to them and they see them as somehow different from them. And sometimes there's a grain of truth to that, because wealthy people, even within the church, at times want to communicate that they somehow *are* different.

In response, rather than getting to know them and ministering to them, pastors often ignore them... until a capital campaign begins. And then, suddenly, pastors want these Christians of capacity to freely give of themselves to the church, even though the church has not given itself freely to them.

As a former pastor myself, I don't want to see this happen. I want Christians of capacity—just like every other member of Christ's body—to discover his or her God-given purpose in the kingdom of God.

So then... what *should* a pastor do with believers of means?

Focus on the Relationship

I deal with a lot of small ministries, especially relatively new ones. Most of them don't know how to relate to wealthy individuals. They feel totally uncomfortable about how to proceed. I often find myself helping them through the conversation by focusing first on the relationship, not on their need or my money.

> *Pastor, if you can help liberate the generosity of the Christians of capacity in your congregation by encouraging them to give in the areas that they feel passionate about, then you will help create a liberality in other areas of their lives, too.*

One group has been chasing me for years. "You're doing great work," I tell them, "but it is not the mission of our foundation." And then they express grave concern that I seem to have no interest in putting the Bible into the hands of people around the world.

Pastors can have a similar skewed attitude. When I talk to them about major donors, I say, "You have the greatest opportunity to impact people of wealth in your congregation by first *being their pastor*. You have entry that normally comes without suspicion. Often when a parachurch organization calls them, immediately the barriers go up. They think, *You just want to get something from me.* Pastor, you're in a position to *give* something to them, but if the only time you ever see them is when you want something, then you're shooting yourself in the foot."

Pastor, if you can help liberate the generosity of the Christians of capacity in your congregation by encouraging them to give in the areas that *they* feel passionate about, then you will help create a liberality in other areas of their lives, too. And your church will benefit from the spillover effect.

Think of a classic scene from *Miracle on 34th Street*. At the very beginning of the movie, Macy's hires an elderly man named Kris Kringle as the store Santa. When children and adults approach him to ask about this toy or that present, he sometimes replies, "Oh, they don't have that here at Macy's, but if you go over to Gimbels…" and he starts sending people to a competitor.

When the department manager learns what Kringle is doing, he wants to fire him, but then a customer says, "What is happening at this store? Your Santa is sending customers to Gimbels! I can't figure it out—but I know I'm coming back here." In the story, Macy's wins over loyal customers by convincing them that it has their best interest at heart, even if it seems to be hurting its own interests in the process.

One of the many great gurus of fund development says that for every ask, there should be at least seven contacts without an ask. People will care about you if they know you care about them. My friend Jim Burns, founder of Homeword, illustrates the idea.

Jim hired a fund development company to do a survey of his ministry's key donors. When the company asked, "Why do you support Homeword?" almost without exception, the donors replied, "Because of Jim."

"And what does Homeword do?"

"Well, we're not really certain."

Jim had become like a pastor to these people; he's probably better at it than I ever was. He officiates at their children's weddings and at family funerals. He makes himself available to everybody for all kinds of ministry occasions.

When Homeword prepared to launch a radio program, Jim had to learn to go to meetings with board members, do presentations, and "make the ask." But he told his board, "There are two people I will never ask." I was one of them.

After a long time of watching Jim do real ministry, I approached him and said, "Jim, you have earned the right to ask."

That's the power of faithful relationship. And if you're a pastor, you're in a unique position to build strong, genuine relationships with the Christians of capacity in your church.

A Relationship Based on Call

I have two friends who both head up major youth ministries. One calls me once a year, the token annual phone catch-up to keep in touch with donors. After fifteen minutes, the call always ends with an appeal for support. The other friend, who lives nearby, takes a genuine interest in my needs. He offers a friendship that includes coffees and lunches, all without appeals.

To whom do you think I give the most?

Who do you think may spur me to go the extra mile in giving?

Which model of relationship do you suppose is the more popular?

The first thing a major donor is going to wonder is this: *Do you love me for me or for my money?*

As a pastor, your role with donors differs somewhat from the nonprofit executive, because your relationship is not based primarily on money (or at least it had better not be). In the nonprofit world, someone usually must give a gift before the director will have anything to do with him or her. You have a relationship, not based upon giving, but upon call.

Your people view you as a pastor/shepherd. You have natural entrée to them. You are able to visit them without making them feel you're doing your money dance. Take advantage of that.

Can They Trust You?

An old fund-raising adage says, "People give to people." In fact, however, people give to people *whom they trust.* Very few individuals will give their money to an investment broker they don't know personally or haven't connected with through a trusted peer.

Pastors often make the mistake of believing that simply because someone is a member of their church, they will automatically give their money. That is true only to a point. They will give what they think they need to give, but if you are to get their extra-mile giving, you will have to go about the task differently. Why?

Church membership alone doesn't give Christians of capacity

enough guarantees that their money will be used wisely. In some situations, wealthy people believe that the church and nonprofits are often the *worst* places to invest their *real* money. So what do they look for?

First and foremost, they look for *integrity*. Do you and the church leadership deliver what you promise? Are you fiscally responsible and do you take responsibility for all your actions? Are you true to your word? Do you use gifts in line with the purpose for which they were given, or do you play shell games? Major donors are like elephants, with long memories. They will let you burn them only once.

Second, do you display the kind of *character* they can trust? Does it appear that most of your new programs simply promote issues that favor you? If your church needs a new educational building and you want a new office, for which do you fight? If you expect your people to give sacrificially, do you? Remember the investor's slogan: "Never risk your own money on people who are unwilling to risk theirs."

Do people see you as *trustworthy*? Are you a visionary or merely a dreamer? Do you hold yourself accountable to your actions? Do you have a board that will hold you accountable?

Pastors who earn the trust of their parishioners tend to gain their support, regardless of the individual's financial status.

What Kind of Leader Are You?

I once met a guy who worked at a computer store. The first time I spoke with him, he could not help me, but he told me where I could go to get what I needed.

Can you guess where I went the next time I had an issue with my computer? I went straight back to him, because I knew he would help me to fix my problem. The same principle holds at church.

Pastor, the days when major donors invested only in organizations or a particular brand of church are gone. Today, they look for effective, high-quality, and trusted leadership.

Are you that kind of leader?

31

GET CREATIVE (HE DID!)

I n 2008 our church, the very church where I had pastored for a dozen years, began a building campaign. Susie and I wanted to use our resources in a constructive and creative way, so we decided to finance the construction loan at 2 percent in order to save the church on finance charges. Of course, when you do such a thing, there is always the risk of "What if they don't raise all the money to pay you back?"

Well, that is exactly what happened.

Knowing that we already had given mightily to the capital campaign, I didn't feel ready to up the ante by forgiving the outstanding debt. I had no desire to create a sense of dependency, where the church came to expect that we always would come to the rescue. Since we had lent foundation dollars to fund the construction, we had a decision to make, knowing that if the church had to finance the outstanding balance with another lender, it would put the operating budget in a big hole.

When I talked to my foundation's board about what the church might do to make up the difference, one board member suggested, "Since it's foundation money anyway and it's for mission purposes, why don't we do a matching missions grant? For every dollar they give to missions, we'll forgive two dollars of the note."

In discussing the idea with our pastor, we identified seven ministries that aligned with the visions of both church and foundation—three locally and four internationally, as well as expanding the church's outreach to the community. We believed and hoped that our fellow church members would express far more enthusiasm about funding mission work than repaying debt. And so we began bringing the targeted ministries into the church to describe their work.

The church had three years to repay the debt by giving to the designated mission projects. By December 2012, with just six months to go, the church still had to raise about $600,000 to satisfy the $1.2 million debt. Since we're a church of 550 members, that figure represented almost 80 percent of the church's annual budget—a big number! Given that the church had decided to challenge its people to give new mission dollars on top of their normal giving, I went to my pastor and said, "Bill, I don't know how we're going to raise this much in six months. We need to start talking." I suggested that we might extend the matching grant after June 1, but it would be a one-for-one match instead of a two-for-one.

In response, the congregation put on a full-scale creative blitz. Over the next six months, the church put together several significant events, including:

- A sold-out golf tournament
- A Super Bowl party
- A 5K/10K run at the park across the street, in partnership with a neighboring Catholic church. We invited the community and about fifteen hundred people showed up.

- A movie-themed *Casablanca* night, for which the church decorated the whole patio and had a wine auction. Practically all the party's expenses were paid for ahead of time and nonmembers accounted for a third of the participants.

Each of these events served a purpose, one that we carefully explained each time: "We're trying to impact our world with the love of Jesus Christ through our missions outreach."

People packed both Sunday services on June 1, eager to know how we did. New gifts came in that morning from enthusiastic donors, and the animated crowds waited for the counters to do their work. Had we reached our goal? At a lunch celebration on the patio immediately following the Sunday services, we would announce the results.

> *People always go beyond themselves if they can believe in and join something bigger than themselves.*

It took about an hour before the accounting team came out, holding a five-foot check made out to Sacred Harvest. A big cheer went up from all parties; we had fallen just $60,000 short of the goal. In six short months, the church had raised $570,000, which meant that with the two-for-one matching grant, the church had to raise just $30,000 more. We were almost totally debt-free!

One young mom called out, "You know, we can do it! I'm going to call my brothers, who weren't here this morning."

A core group of about a dozen people suddenly streamed into the church offices and started getting on the phone to call their friends and family members. We even had church members calling in from vacation, trying to find out how things went. When they heard how close we were, they gave even more.

By five o'clock that night, the church had its $30,000.

If you talk with Pastor Bill, he says, "That experience has changed the DNA of our congregation." But note that it wasn't all about our gift; our gift merely encouraged people to get involved, many who had never chosen to hop aboard before. The whole thing created a level of excitement that empowered the people of the church to get the job done, directed and energized by a clear purpose and vision.

Pastor Bill keeps asking, "How can we recapture that excitement?"

People always go beyond themselves if they can believe in and join something bigger than themselves. I use the word *sexy* to describe something that captures both the imagination and the heart, something with a strong heartbeat and a solid brainwave. To become truly passionate about a cause, we need to get both head and heart deeply involved.

And *that* takes creativity.

Can a Fish Pay Taxes?

Getting creative in the way you use your resources takes place at two levels.

It starts by beginning to utilize *all* your wealth, that is to say, the whole investment portfolio God has given to you. God wants you to invest more for Him than just your time and dollars and abilities! What about your connections, your influence, your leadership, your enthusiasm, and even your mistakes?

Second, it takes getting creative and imaginative with your wealth. We serve an amazingly creative God, and as people made in His image, we have the opportunity to reflect back to Him a little of His own divine ingenuity. Sometimes, this can even get a little comical.

Do you remember what happened when the apostle Peter came to Jesus, worried about how they'd pay a two-drachma temple tax? Before he could even ask about it, Jesus said to him, "Go to the lake and throw out your line. Take the first fish you catch; open its mouth and you will find a four-drachma coin. Take it and give it to them for my tax and yours" (Matthew 17:27).

Now, that's creativity. (With a little divine humor thrown in, I think.)

I can't tell people how to find coins in a fish's mouth, but I can tell them how some others have gotten creative in their use of the resources God has given to them.

My late mother-in-law, Jeanette Segerstrom, owned a couple of beautiful homes on Newport Bay, plus a forty-eight-foot yacht once owned by my father-in-law. For the most part, those resources existed solely for her family's use. But one day I accompanied Susie and her sister to speak with Jeanette about an idea. Susie described the need for a place where pastors and their spouses could come away to get renewed and refreshed for ministry. Recognizing that pastors and their spouses are very often underpaid and underappreciated, Mom gladly offered the use of her million-dollar homes. Then she enthusiastically added, "Be sure to use Daddy's boat." We never imagined that by involving Mom in the mission, she would get equally excited by it. Even better, others soon got excited and stimulated by the vision. Within weeks of telling friends at church what we wanted to do for pastors and spouses, a group approached us to see if they could participate in the ministry. So we put together teams of excited cooks and servers to serve dinner every night of these four-day retreats.

You don't have to be a millionaire to do this kind of thing; you just have to be willing and a little creative. I heard of a young boy who decided to befriend a new neighbor kid by inviting him into his home to play Nintendo. The relationship that that resulted from that simple invitation became the bed-rock upon which that new neighbor now regularly attends church and youth group.

When you see a need that you can't meet, don't just brush it off. Get a little creative. Look into the wealth of the relationships that God has given you and see if the individuals you know might be able to meet that need.

You might even ask how you can use your own professional skills to be a blessing.

A close friend has a daughter who loves working with deaf children. She went to college to learn sign language and became a teacher to the deaf. She began a great career but then some-thing even greater happened. God gave her a vision to take in deaf foster children, a demographic that's pretty hard to place. But this young woman wanted to teach these children how much they are loved, both by her and by God.

Her first case involved two little black girls, the daughters of a drug addict. The three-year-old was wild and rebellious, while the one-year-old was deaf and developmentally far behind. Social workers doubted she would ever walk.

Two years later, the littlest one is not only signing, but walking. The oldest now has bright, happy eyes, and both little girls have come to love Jesus. In fact, when the foster mom needs to discipline them, all she has to tell them is, "If you don't behave, you can't have a Bible story at bedtime." They immediately straighten up.

Bring on the Creativity!

We don't lack many resources for God's kingdom today; all of heaven and earth belongs to God and He has entrusted a good share of it to us. Neither do we usually lack desire. What we lack is imagination, creativity, and resourcefulness in using our wealth in ways that bring blessing.

Like the explorers of *Star Trek*, our commission is to seek out new ways and new means to bless others through whatever God has given to us. Whatever you have—a love for motorcycles, a house at the beach, a knack for solving problems—use it creatively as a faithful steward of God.

God has given you a fabulous brain to find innovative ways of using your wealth to honor Him and help your neighbor. So have fun and *get creative*!

32

WHAT'S IN A NAME?

I f someone were to ask you to name your most valuable
asset, how would you respond? Probably you would choose
something based upon what you hold most dear—a home, a car,
a career, a degree or professional credentials, even a favorite
body part.

But what if you were to ask *God* the same question? How
do you think He'd respond?

I'm quite sure He wouldn't point to the vast oceans or to the
great sea creatures churning their depths; those things provide
mere whispers of His grandeur (Job 26:8–14).

Nor would He name the earth; that's just His footstool
(Isaiah 66:1).

Nor would He designate the heavens; to Him, they're like
an old tent (Psalm 104:2).

I doubt He'd mention even the entire universe, since He
plans to roll up the whole thing like a worn-out scroll. It will
vanish like dry paper tossed in a furnace (Isaiah 51:6; 2 Peter
3:12).

So what *does* God consider His most valuable asset? He
doesn't leave us in suspense.

A Name Above Every Other

God tells us in the second of the Ten Commandments, "You shall not take the name of the LORD your God in vain" (Exodus 20:7). We avoid taking God's name "in vain" not just by refusing to use it as a curse word, but by living in a way that protects His good reputation. As His people, called by His name, we refuse to live in ways that misrepresent Him or put Him in a negative or false light. His name, after all, is "far above… every name that is named, not only in this age but also in the one to come" (Ephesians 1:21, ESV). So the Psalmist said to the Lord, "You have exalted above all things your name and your word" (Psalm 138:2, NIV).

> *When God blesses us with a good name,*
> *guess what comes with it? The ability to*
> *influence others for good.*

The Lord insists that His most important asset is His *name*. But why should God's name be so important to Him? Why would He exalt it above all things?

In the Bible, God's name stands for everything good and holy and majestic and awesome and glorious about Him. When He connects His name to something, that something becomes glorious by extension. So when He surprised everyone by connecting His name to the inconsequential people of Israel, it was a fearsome thing:

> Bring my sons from afar and my daughters from the ends of the earth—everyone who is called by my name, whom I created for my glory, whom I formed and made. (Isaiah 43:6–7, NIV).

Our Most Important Asset

So then, what's *our* most important asset, from God's perspective? Not surprisingly, He puts our *name* at the top of the list. That's why He protects it with the eighth commandment: "You shall not give false testimony against your neighbor" (Exodus 20:16). In his Large Catechism, Martin Luther explains the idea this way:

> Over and above our own body, spouse, and temporal possessions, we have yet another treasure, namely, honor and good report [the illustrious testimony of an upright and unsullied name and reputation], with which we cannot dispense. For it is intolerable to live among men in open shame and general contempt. God does not wish the reputation, good name, and upright character of our neighbor to be taken away or diminished any more than his money and possessions, that every one may stand in his integrity before wife, children, servants and neighbors.

All of us know from personal experience the results of having a questionable name or reputation. A sullied name becomes a stumbling block to our relationships, our business activities, and yes, even to our self-esteem. A ruined name compromises our every effort to succeed or achieve in this life.

A good name, by contrast, has the opposite effect. In Genesis 12:2, God tells Abraham, "I will make your name great, and you will be a blessing." Having a good (or even great) name is not only about preserving your self-image. God wants *you* to use *your* good name to bring blessing to others!

When we talk about stewarding our resources, we usually have a pretty clear understanding of our allotments of time, talent, and treasures. But how many of us think about "tithing our influence," as a friend of mine used to say?

When God blesses us with a good name, guess what comes with it?

The ability to influence others for good.

Use Your Name Well

Right after I resigned my call as a pastor, Susie and I began to get involved on a greater level with our charitable ambitions. One night, we attended a fund-raising event for a local inner-city ministry. By this point, our capacity to give had exceeded our vision. Since we had not yet fully formulated our mission and vision for giving, we decided to consider potential opportunities with a fairly broad net. While I knew very little about the beneficiary of that evening's fund-raiser, even then

I knew enough to know that it's unwise to give to anyone or anything about which you're fairly ignorant.

At the end of a powerful and moving presentation, the ministry listed the names of its key sponsors. Among the names we recognized a couple for whom we had tremendous respect; we also knew this couple gave their money wisely. Instantly, our confidence in the ministry reached a level far higher than when we had entered the room. Later that night, we made a gift to the organization.

What's in a name? Quite a lot, actually.

In our hometown area of Southern California, Susie and I know this legacy of a good name all too well. We know it because God has given her family, the Segerstroms, a "great and respected name" in Orange County. And so we continually ask ourselves, "How can we use the Segerstrom name in a way that doesn't prostitute it, but which gives us the proper ability to influence others for kingdom causes that we love and support?" This is what I mean by tithing one's influence.

When we decide to support some ministry or organization, we normally seek anonymity in the gift, unless the ministry or organization believes that by using our name, it can encourage others to add their own support. We never seek naming rights for the causes we support, unless it becomes clear that by lending our name to the venture, we can tithe our influence.

Not long ago, our alma mater, Azusa Pacific University, approached us about securing the naming rights for the school's new science center. We already had made a large commitment to the fund-raising campaign, so when a representative asked if we would like naming rights, the question shocked me. I knew

that naming rights usually come with a requirement that the donors supply at least 40 percent of the cost for the entire project.

"I don't have that kind of money to give," I replied.

The representative quickly restated his query. "No, no," he
said, "if you can double your commitment, then we will give
you the naming rights."

Now, the last thing anyone would want to name such a
fabulous new facility is the Perry Science Center. Who on earth
would have the slightest idea about the Perry of the title? But
if the school were to call it the Segerstrom Science Center, well,
that could mean something. Young people in Orange County
who grew up hearing the name (as in the Segerstrom Center
for the Arts or Segerstrom Avenue in Santa Ana) might find
the name meaningful, and so it could give them one more in-
centive to choose APU.

With that in mind, I approached my wife and her sister Sally,
also an APU alumna, and told them about the naming rights
possibility. To their great credit, they both agreed to double
the combined gift for the center—but almost in unison they
said, "We don't want the naming rights." Though I beamed
with pride over their willingness to give without recognition,
I countered with a different perspective.

"I think there are two good reasons why you should consider taking advantage of putting your family name on the
new science center," I said. "First, this would be the very first
legacy gift of the family for a building with a distinctively
Christian purpose. Second, think of the influence that having
the Segerstrom name on the center could have in encouraging students from Orange Country to decide to attend Azusa

Pacific." They both saw the logic, agreed with my reasoning, and consented to have the university call the new building the Segerstrom Science Center.

What's in a name? Sometimes, a great deal.

A Favorable Influence

All of us have a great name in at least some areas of our lives. While some individuals definitely have larger areas of influence than others, size doesn't matter on this issue, as they say.

What matters is using your name in a way that favorably influences—not manipulates!—others to join you in a worthy cause for the kingdom.

33

MAZEL TOV

When Ronald Reagan kicked off his successful bid for the presidency on November 13, 1979, he did so with a rousing speech from the ballroom of the Hilton Hotel in New York City. He wanted both the nation and the world to hear how his upbeat outlook could help turn around an attitude of defeatism that he saw crippling the country. Toward the end of his speech he said:

> The citizens of this great nation want leadership—yes—but not a "man on a white horse" demanding obedience to his commands. They want someone who believes they can "begin the world over again." A leader who will unleash their great strength and remove the roadblocks government has put in their way. I want to do that more than anything I've ever wanted. And it's something that I believe with God's help I can do.

Whatever you think of Reagan's policies, his two terms as president brought major changes to the nation and the world, including the end of the Cold War. Reagan meant what he said in his kickoff speech, and it set the tone for his whole administration.

Like Reagan, leaders and politicians of every stripe carefully superintend the kickoff event designed to announce a political candidacy or some new social movement. They want observers to get just the right idea about who they are and what they intend to accomplish. They use the event to announce to the world, "Here I am!"

When Jesus Christ kicked off His own public ministry, He did so not from a ballroom in a metropolis but at a wedding in a small town. And yet, in a very real sense, what He said and did there announced to the world, "Here I am and this is what I'm about."

While the world remembers Jesus as a teacher and (maybe) a miracle worker, Christians worship Him as the Son of God, their savior who died for their sins and rose from the dead to bring them eternal life. That's quite a résumé for anyone! So how did Jesus choose to begin His public ministry? How did He craft His initial appearance to set the tone for all that would follow?

He attended a wedding. And when the unfortunate hosts ran out of wine—an unforgivable faux pas in those days—He made sure the festivities didn't go sour by turning water into the very best wine the banquet master had ever tasted.

Imagine: Jesus announced His divine presence to this needy world by *keeping a party going!*

No Two-Buck Chuck Here

When the wedding ran out of wine, Jesus could have ignored the need or provided the unprepared hosts with Two-Buck Chuck (a cheap wine)—but instead He supplied the best wine imaginable. John tells us that when the master of the banquet tasted the water made into wine, he immediately called the bridegroom aside and said, "Everyone brings out the choice wine first and then the cheaper wine after the guests have had too much to drink, but you have saved the best till now" (John 2:10).

He didn't mean it as a compliment! But it was—although not one intended for the host. More than two millennia later, the banquet master's words continue to give tribute to Jesus and tell us that He loves to give good gifts to undeserving people for their enjoyment. (And our Lord didn't slip a tract into the water jars that said, "Compliments of Jesus of Nazareth—now repent.")

It means something that Jesus Christ began His public ministry by attending a wedding, where He quietly turned ordinary water into great wine. As His opening statement to the world, it tells me that Jesus is all about grace, about giving, about surprises, and about celebration. While He had to navigate through some very dark moments, the darkest of all at the cross, He began His ministry in sunshine and He will bring that ministry to a bright fulfillment in a city so filled with His glory that it won't even need the sun.

And by the way, this wine thing wasn't a one-time occurrence. At the dinner we call the Last Supper, He invited His disciples to drink from a cup He had blessed and then said to them, "This is my blood of the covenant, which is poured out for many for the forgiveness of sins. I tell you, I will not drink of this fruit of the vine from now on until that day when I drink it anew with you in my Father's kingdom" (Matthew 26:28–29). That's a party I'd like to attend! I don't think He'll be serving Two-Buck Chuck there, either.

Acres of Love

Acres of Love, a Christian ministry in South Africa, runs about twenty-seven group homes (called Forever Homes) for abandoned or orphaned children. Twenty-three are located in Johannesburg and three or four are in Cape Town, where we helped the ministry expand several years ago.

Each home cares for anywhere from eight to ten children. All of the homes have a house mother or house parents and a housekeeper/cook. That way, the house mother can remain totally devoted to the children.

Although many of these children suffer from AIDS, the ministry does not refuse anyone due to the nature of their disability. In fact, the group considers it a calling of God to help those with severe disabilities. The ministry lovingly takes in these children and gives them its best.

And I do mean best. These homes rival anything you could find in Orange County. Acres of Love buys great houses in nice neighborhoods and their children attend the best public or private schools, as needed. The children get their medical care from private physicians, not at the public hospitals. (If you've seen a majority world public hospital, you know what I'm talking about.)

> *Jesus wants Christians of capacity to celebrate, to enjoy life, and to look for ways to help others to celebrate. When they do so, they honor their Master.*

A couple of years ago as I traveled with Gerda Audagnotti, the founder of Acres of Love, something dawned on me. "What happens to the disabled kids when they age out at eighteen?" I wondered aloud. "Where do they go?" We have two deaf girls in a home we sponsor. "What happens to our girls and to all the others?" I asked.

Some of these homes have children who suffer from cerebral palsy and use wheelchairs. These children will never be able to live on their own or take care of themselves.

"Yes," she said, "I know that's something that we'll have to deal with."

"When you get to that point, let us know," I replied. "We'd like to participate in that."

Little did I know what our participation would look like.

The wine region of Africa is located in Stellenbosch, near Cape Town. Stellenbosch makes Napa, California, look like a dump. Very high, rugged mountains rise up from the sides of a beautiful valley, almost like the Tetons. The valley itself looks lush and green, dotted with white Dutch-style homes surrounded by vineyards. It lacks the clutter of Napa. If you've ever driven through Napa, you know it can take half an hour just to get out of town, and you won't see a vineyard for who knows how long. Not so in Stellenbosch.

225

Gerda is in the process of buying a manor house on four acres. The property lies just a few minutes from town and will serve as a home for those with disabilities as well as the central gathering spot for all the Forever Homes in Cape Town.

Gerda wants to provide a facility where these disabled children can remain active. "I don't want them just sitting around doing nothing," she declares. She plans to bring in cottage industries of various types; you could call it the Goodwill of South Africa. Some of these children are capable of working outside of the complex, and since it's only a short drive into town, staff can take them there to work at jobs suitable for someone confined to a wheelchair.

"You know," Gerda told me, "maybe I'll have a coffee shop and have a little bakery in the back, and some of the kids can learn to do that."

Without question, Gerda has a particular direction she wants to go. We'll see where God leads, but we're already very happy with the quality of life that the ministry enables these children to enjoy. But one thing we know for sure already: Gerda doesn't give her kids Two-Buck Chuck, any more than Jesus would.

Let's Be Glad

At the end of modern Jewish weddings, the bridegroom breaks a glass under his foot and the guests shout, "Mazel tov!" This Yiddish phrase essentially means, "We're glad this good thing has happened to you!" (And it sounds a lot better than our weak "Congratulations!")

Cana reminds me that Jesus wants Christians of capacity to celebrate, to enjoy life and to look for ways to help others to celebrate. When they do so, they honor their Master, who at Cana performed the first of His miraculous signs and "thus revealed His glory," prompting His disciples to "put their faith in Him" (John 2:11).

What kind of Cana can you envision in your own future?

34

JOY IN THE JOURNEY

Our foundation has underwritten about eighty grants in the Philippines, but one of my favorites will always remain the one we did with a ministry called A Salaam a Likum. The ministry works with the Badjao, one of thirteen Muslim tribal groups in Mindanao. The Badjao occupy the lowest possible social rung. In the Philippines they are considered by many to be the untouchables, similar to the Dalits of India.

Most people don't realize that even the poor have a caste system. Yes, some poor take pride over other poor: "I have a cement floor, you have only a dirt floor." The Badjao are also called Sea Gypsies, because they're always squatting over the shoreline and building stick cities.

We did our work with A Salaam a Likum in the town of Santa Cruz, where we helped build a community center in the middle of a group of stick shacks. When we visited Santa Cruz for the dedication of the facility, we heard about Sister Serena, who had served the Badjao for forty years. We learned she had longed and prayed for just such a place to serve her people. On the day of the dedication, we discovered that the nun she lives with had repeatedly told her, "Why don't you give up on these people? Your dream is never going to happen! They have nothing and they will always have nothing." But Sister Serena never gave up on her call to serve the Badjao, or on her dream of having a community center.

What a blessing it was to know that we helped to fulfill a forty-year-old prayer request! It quite literally brought tears to my eyes. You can't help but love Sister Serena. She is spunky and full of life and one of the happiest people you could ever hope to meet. She just exudes the joy of the Lord.

Yes, Sister Serena suffered a lot over those forty long years when she saw her dream go unfulfilled. Nevertheless, she also knew a great deal about how God wants us to experience joy in the journey—and she knew it long before we opened the community center.

The Call to Enjoyment

All of us have had the unpleasant experience of giving a gift only because someone "guilted" us into it. Besides the fact that such a gift brings no joy, our attitude prompts thoughts like, *Okay, what is the least I have to give in order to satisfy my obligation?*

Guilt turns us all into misers and bean counters obsessed with just getting by.

On the other hand, when we give a gift because we desire to give it, we give not only with joy but also without measure.

Serious Christians understand spiritual responsibility. They accept the sense of duty and commitment that comes with being a fully committed follower of Jesus. We probably have a harder time, though, trying to grasp joy. Duty, approached in the wrong way, can become so burdensome that it can squeeze all joy out of life.

> *The key to finding joy is to live in*
> *whatever gives God joy.*

I suspect this warped mind-set comes, at least in part, from an old piety that emphasizes an ascetic viewpoint. It says, for example, that if you buy anything new, your action reeks of materialism. It also implies that if you ever do buy a new thing, then you must do everything in your power to show that you don't enjoy it, out of fear that others will perceive it as an idol in your life.

The same skewed perspective suggests that you should not enjoy the physical aspect of marriage. "Sex needs to be purposeful," this line of thinking goes. "It's not for enjoyment. Sex is for procreation and nothing more. Therefore you do your duty with the lights out so that you don't get too aroused, only enough to get the job done. The Song of Songs is really about Jesus's ministry, nothing else."

How ridiculous.

The fact is that God created a whole lot of this world to be enjoyed. "A man can do nothing better than to eat and drink and find satisfaction in his work," declares the Bible. "This too, I see, is from the hand of God, for without Him, who can eat or find enjoyment? To the person who pleases Him, God gives wisdom, knowledge and happiness" (Ecclesiastes 2:24–26). The apostle Paul echoed the same sentiment in the New Testament when he wrote that God "richly provides us with everything for our enjoyment" (1 Timothy 6:17).

Our wealth? Sure. The physically intimate side of marriage? Certainly. Paul insists that God *richly* provides us with *everything* for our *enjoyment*. Sounds pretty global to me.

The reformer John Calvin hardly earned a reputation as a good-time Charlie. Yet this meticulous scholar also recognized that God created innumerable things for our enjoyment: "Did God create food only to provide for necessity [nutrition] and not also for delight and good cheer? So too the purpose of clothing apart from necessity [protection] was comeliness and decency. In grasses, trees, and fruits, apart from their various uses, there is beauty of appearance and pleasantness of fragrance. ...Did He not, in short, render many things attractive to us, apart from their necessary use?"

Jeremy Taylor, a seventeenth-century English cleric (sometimes called the Shakespeare of Divines for his lyrical manner of expression), once said, "God threatens terrible things if we will not be happy." He probably had in mind a text like Deuteronomy 28:47-48, where Moses told the people of Israel:

> Because you did not serve the LORD your God joyfully and gladly in the time of prosperity, therefore in hunger and thirst, in nakedness and dire poverty, you will serve the enemies the LORD sends against you. He will put an iron yoke on your neck until He has destroyed you.

Joy is a serious business, indeed!

The contemporary Messianic Church Arising has given a lot of thought to the biblical idea of first fruits and its connection to joy. It says:

- The biblical calendar has days for fasting and repentance, but also days for feasting and being extravagant, for enjoying to the fullest every blessing God has given.
- All of life is a gracious gift from God, and God desires His children to enjoy His blessings. God commanded His people to take a special tithe of their income and spend it on feasting extravagantly (Deuteronomy 14:25–26).
- Eat, drink, and be thankful, because life is a gift from God (Ecclesiastes 3:13).

Christians have every right—and every duty—to rejoice and be happy, as every other follower of Jesus. And the key to finding joy is to live in whatever gives God joy.

Finding Joy

Remember the 1981 movie *Chariots of Fire*? The film recalls Eric Liddell, an English Olympian in the 1920s and the son of missionaries to China. He returned to England for a time to raise support for his family's work. But Eric also loved to run; he saw it as a gift from God and he used that gift as a platform to glorify God. When his sister tried to talk him out of going to the Olympics because of the great missionary work still remaining, he responded with these memorable words: "When I run, I feel God's pleasure."

I heard a similar story of a Christian businessman who sold his business at a nice profit. Since he had a lifelong dream to buy a small yacht, he did so after he sold his business.

But something strange and haunting happened to him the day after he bought the boat. He began to suffer what I call

"Christian buyer's blues." We all know the feeling of buyer's blues, the regret that comes after some impulsive purchase. Christian buyer's blues adds the thought, *Maybe I spent too much on myself.* That was the arrow stuck in this businessman's conscience. Although he had given generously to Christian causes, he still fell under Schindler's curse, thinking he could have done so much more if he hadn't bought the boat.

Not knowing for certain if what he felt was genuine guilt brought on by the Holy Spirit, he decided to pray about it. If in prayer God would confirm that he ought to give up the boat, he would do so. But after days of praying, he finally heard that quiet inner voice telling him, "Use it for My glory." He believed he had heard from God.

The next day, he called the local YMCA and asked the director if he had any need of a yacht to take inner-city children out on the ocean to explore the wonders of God's creation. To his surprise, he got an immediate and enthusiastic response: "We do!"

At that moment, his boat was "reborn." As he offered it in service to his neighbor and to his God—and yes, for his family's enjoyment—it got baptized as a vessel for noble use. And like Eric Liddell, he felt the pleasure of his Lord run through his whole being. He found not only purpose, he found joy.

And we can, too.

35

THE LAVISHNESS OF GOD

I used to have a fairly utilitarian view of God. I thought of
Him as a heavenly Scrooge, measuring out His blessings by
the thimbleful, giving no more than the minimum requirement.
He seemed a lot like my grandmother, who every year gave
me underwear for Christmas.

I could almost see Him, shaking His head and sorrowfully
telling me, "No, Steve, you don't need an extra twenty bucks
to spend on frivolities. But here's some nice broccoli for you."

At Bible school in the early '70s, I lived essentially from hand
to mouth. I had basic transportation, a ten-year-old car with a
gas-efficient six-cylinder engine. I ate frozen dinners and drank
a lot of water. I don't remember buying a single ticket to see a
movie. But really, none of those things bothered me, because I
couldn't afford anything else after paying my tithe.

In those days, Christian music was just getting revved up:
Love Song, Children of the Day, 2nd Chapter of Acts. Maranatha
music had changed the world for me, but my bare-bones car
had neither a cassette player nor an eight-track player. Oh, how
I longed to listen to Christian music when I drove around!

So I began to pray, timidly, that God would somehow provide me with a tape player. But the whole time I prayed, I felt as though I had crossed the line. Who did I think I was to ask for a mere want? I could only imagine God clucking His tongue and saying to me, "What do you want, egg in your beer?"—a question I heard occasionally from my ex-marine father. It implied that I was being a little too greedy, always desiring something more than what was necessary. Try as I might, I couldn't shake the feeling that I had crossed the line. How could I dare ask for steak when I'd already received half a plate of broccoli?

Yet something deep inside encouraged me to hope that, just maybe, it was all right to ask.

A month later, a friend of mine told me he had a cassette player that he no longer needed. He sold it to me for next to nothing. And before I knew it, I found myself motoring down Southern California streets to the groovy sounds of 2nd Chapter of Acts.

Could it be that God is like any other father who delights in doing special things for his children? Could the Lord actually *look* for ways to bring joy and delight into their lives? Even to supplying a tape player?

Why not?

"Which of you," Jesus asked, "if your son asks for bread, will give him a stone? Or if he asks for a fish, will give him a snake? If you, then, though you are evil, know how to give good gifts to your children, how much more will your Father in heaven give good gifts to those who ask him!" (Matthew 7:9–11).

I learned eventually that Jesus's words simply built on what God had revealed about Himself long before. I heard God say things I'd never imagined He would ever say, especially to me. Things like, "Open wide your mouth and I will fill it" (Psalm 81:10, NIV).

Many earnest Christians, I know, question the lavishness of God. Although we dutifully confess that His mercies are new every morning, how often do we suspect that God has, in fact, put limits on His grace? How many times can He forgive us, we wonder, before He decides we've taken advantage of Him once too often?

In my younger days, I often struggled with that question: *How many times can God forgive me, especially for the same thing?* And just as the devil used Scripture to tempt Jesus in the wilderness, trying to distort God's nature and obscure the Lord's will, so he did to me. One day, in the midst of this internal debate over the limits to God's grace, I stumbled across a passage in the Gospels where Peter asked Jesus, "Lord, how often should we forgive, seven times?" Jesus replied, "I tell you, not seven times, but seven times seventy" (Matthew 18:22, NASB).

In that instant, the idea got planted in my brain that the measure of God's grace far exceeds our own. Although in an especially magnanimous moment we might feel willing to forgive up to seven times (and that's probably stretching it), Jesus says that true, divine-like mercy involves a willingness to forgive up to *490* times! The thought staggered me. I remember thinking, *When we are born, we are all given 490 tokens of forgiveness to use, at any time we please. Wow!*

And instantly, an oily voice inside my head said to me, "Steve, you are at 491."

One step over the line, bud.

A line from a then-popular song summed up my problem. The words seemed to summarize my difficulty (in general, not in the details): "One toke over the line, sweet Jesus, one toke over the line. ...Who do you love? I hope it's me."*

We all struggle with the idea of a God who lavishes us with His grace, blessings, and forgiveness. Somehow we can hardly believe that we serve a God who takes delight in providing for His children, not only whatever they need, but even nonessential gifts that seem a little over the top. We struggle to accept that we belong to a God of lavishness.

But that's exactly what we see, time and again, in the miracles of Jesus.

When He fed the five thousand, couldn't He have fed everyone without creating such excess? I mean, twelve extra baskets of bread (see Matthew 14:20)? Or later, when He fed the four thousand, did He really need to whip up enough food to fill seven basketfuls after the crowd had eaten its fill (see Matthew 15:37)?

When His disciples spent the good part of a day in a failed attempt to catch fish, Jesus told them to cast their nets on the other side of the boat. When they did, they not only got a haul sufficient for the day, but for a whole week—153 fish in all (John 21:11).

Jesus's healing ministry inspired Matthew to repeatedly employ a couple of words: *every* and *all*. As in, "Jesus went throughout Galilee… healing *every* disease and sickness among

---

* Brewer and Shipley, "One Toke Over the Line," 1971.

the people. News about Him spread *all* over Syria, and people brought to Him *all* who were ill with various diseases, those suffering severe pain, the demon-possessed, those having seizures, and the paralyzed, and He healed them" (Matthew 4:23–24; see also Matthew 8:16, 12:15, 14:36, 15:30).

Even God's spiritual gifts come to us with liberality. Many of the gifts Paul lists in Romans 12—service, encouragement, giving, mercy—represent duties and responsibilities that every Christian bears, without exception. But to some, Christ gives an extra special measure, a gift that far exceeds the norm. Do these believers "deserve" such lavishness? No. He just likes giving lavishly.

That is a lavish God. We don't serve a cheap God nor one who has to watch His pennies!

So if God can delight in lavishing His gifts on us, joyfully providing us far more than the minimum, then why can't we do the same thing with those He calls us to serve?

Our foundation, Sacred Harvest, in partnership with Cure International and the Tim Tebow Foundation, this past year dedicated a brand-new, thirty-bed orthopedic hospital in Mindanao, Philippines, designed to treat curable disabilities of the island's impoverished children. When I saw the completed facility, the quality of finish amazed me. It had a marble entryway and first-world operating rooms (no hand-me-downs). It looked like any hospital in the United States, maybe better than most. As I toured the facility, it seemed just as nice as the Marco Polo, a four-star hotel in Davao, Mindanao.

No doubt some people would question why anyone would build a hospital, designed to serve the poor, that looks as nice

> *If God can delight in lavishing His gifts on us, joyfully providing us far more than the minimum, then why can't we do the same thing with those He calls us to serve?*

as the city's best hotel. Certainly, Cure could have economized on the finishing touches!

But it didn't trouble me at all. I hope and pray that every patient who enters the facility will see its grandeur and beauty and conclude that he or she is worthy of the best that God wants to lavish on them.

Because, you know, that's what He *really* likes to do.

EPILOGUE
THE JOURNEY CONTINUES

After hearing his excited friends discuss how much they enjoyed ice fishing, a young man decided to give it a try. So he bought some gear and early the next morning trudged out to the ice and cut a hole in it. Just as he did so, he heard a loud voice say, "There are no fish under the ice."

Amazed at hearing a voice speaking to him, he wondered if it might be God. He finally convinced himself that he had probably imagined the whole thing, so he got up and started to drill another hole a few yards from the first one.

"There are no fish under the ice," the voice repeated.

Trembling with fear and wonder, the young man replied slowly, "Is that you, God?"

"No," said the voice, "this is the ice rink manager."

Hearing the genuine voice of God can sometimes feel a little tricky for many of us… but most of the time, I doubt it's nearly so complicated as we imagine. If your heart's desire is to use your wealth in a way that honors God and accomplishes His will, He'll get you there. He really will.

I recently heard my pastor say that the Latin term for "obey," *oboedire*, means "to give ear," "to hearken," "to listen." The notion interested me so much that I looked it up, and sure enough, it's true.

A little more research revealed that the primary Greek term in the New Testament for "obey," *hypakouo*, literally means "to hear beneath," while the converse term for "disobey," *parakouo*, literally means "to hear beside." The idea seems to be that when we obey what we hear God say, we put His words on our shoulders and move ahead with them, while when we disobey, we let the divine words go whistling past our ears and continue on our own merry way.

Do you want to find God's will for your life, particularly in regard to how you handle your wealth? In other words, do you want to obey Him? If so, then you need to learn to *listen* intently for His voice and then commit to *do* what He says. You need to hear beneath.

> *The journey for all of us continues until the moment God leads us home.*

To obey God does not mean to look for ways to suffer, as I once thought. It does not mean to choose how you will "sacrifice" for God. It does not mean to imitate what you see your brothers or sisters in Christ doing, although you can certainly learn from them and use their stories for inspiration.

In writing this book, I certainly have not desired that you imitate what Susie and I have done in our own pursuit of God's will for us. Nor do I want to suggest that where you are today is exactly where God will want you in the years to come. I have described a bit of our journey over the last forty years only to encourage you to find your own path, wherever it may lead. I cannot say where our own journey will take us in the next decades. And that journey is far from over! Where we go from here will all depend upon what Susie and I believe to be God's will for our lives… and prayerfully, nothing else. The journey for *all* of us continues until the moment God leads us home.

In a similar way, for both us and for you, finding God's will requires listening for His voice, preferably after we've spent some good time grazing in His Word, the Bible. Sometimes you'll hear that voice in the counsel of wise friends. Sometimes you'll sense it in your circumstances or in a quiet moment in prayer. Don't forget that stuff happens! When that stuff happens to you, listen for His voice in it and then take a step of faith to do whatever you believe is His will for you.

And *relax*. You don't have to fret and worry that you might be hearing from the ice rink manager rather than from God. God has a way of leading people who really want to honor Him, sometimes despite themselves. So try not to agonize over whether you *really* heard God correctly. If you want to please Him more than anything and you desire to honor both Him and His Word, then take that step of faith. Go ahead, take it! And know that His grace will always be there with you.

ACKNOWLEDGMENTS

My life is an imprint of many other lives that have contributed to shaping me into the person I am today. Any strength reflected in this book is a direct result of those who have influenced both my life and Susie's. They have shaped our ability to integrate our faith and wealth in a way that liberates us to joyfully steward our wealth. I've mentioned many of those people in this book: Fred Smith, Ray Lyne, Gary Moore, and others not mentioned but who have had a significant influence on me over the years, including Skye Jethani, Rob Martin, Jim Johnson, Bob Fry, and Terry Parker.

Yet this book never would have come to be at all without the strong encouragement and belief in my message expressed by my dear friends John Townsend and Greg Campbell, nor without the writing assistance of a new friend, Steve Halliday. Steve was essential to the development of this book by working hard to preserve my voice and sense of humor.

Finally, Susie and I want to thank our home congregation, Mission Lutheran Church in Laguna Niguel, California, and our pastor, Bill Snyder, for allowing us simply to be the people God wants us to be.

ABOUT THE AUTHOR

Steven L. Perry graduated from Azusa Pacific University in 1975 with a BA in Religion and in 1979 from Wartburg Theological Seminary. He served from 1979–1984 as associate pastor at Grace Lutheran Church in Huntington Beach, California, and as senior pastor at Mission Lutheran Church in Laguna Niguel, California, from 1984–1996. In 1996 he cofounded the Foundation for Christian Stewardship, now the National Christian Foundation California. Seven years later, in 2003, he founded Sacred Harvest Foundation with his wife, Susie. He currently serves on the boards of Azusa Pacific University, National Christian Foundation California, and Mission Increase Foundation.

Steve met Susie at Azusa Pacific University and the two married on December 27, 1975. Steve and Susie have two married children, Jennifer and Matthew. Jennifer and her husband, Ryan Somers, have two children, Ethan and Danny. Matthew is married to Katherine.

For more information regarding *Living With Wealth Without Losing Your Soul*, go to www.livingwithwealth.org for a complimentary Discussion Guide and suggested Sermon Notes.